HOW TO BLOG FOR MONEY:
9 STRATEGIES TO GET YOUR BLOG EARNING MONEY ONLINE AND OFF

By
Glen Ford

Published By
Training NOW
Mississauga, Canada

Published by TrainingNOW, Mississauga & Oakville, Ontario, Canada
http://www.TrainingNOW.ca
http://www.LearningCreators.com
http://www.howtoblogmoney.com

ISBN (Kindle Edition):   978-0-9867885-7-4
ISBN (Print Edition) :   978-0-9867885-8-1

This book is dedicated to my wife and family
who have put up with so much
and given me so much

Acknowledgements

No book is an island ... well no author is anyway. I want to thank my business partner and editor Paul who helped me a great deal with this book and the video course it grew from. I also want to thank my wife. Lisa, you put up with my spending weeks at a time focused on my books. I may not be ignoring you but I know it seems that way. And to Dafydd and Solenne who have both shown they have writing talent. You poor kids.

Oh yes, and I also want to thank whatever muse it was that got me writing blogs. I will pay you back somehow ...

Table of Contents

SO YOU WANT TO BE RICH   **1**

Possibilities and Promises   1
Who This Book Is For   3
A Note about Income Amounts   4
How This Book Is Arranged   5

START FROM THE SECOND HABIT   **9**

It All Starts with Why   9
Understanding Why   10
Money vs. Ego   12
Money as the Underlying Reason   13
The Effects of Why   16
Getting to Why   19

MODELS, MONEY AND MAYHEM   23

WHAT IS A MODEL AND WHY SHOULD I CARE?   23
SALES MODELS AND PROCESSES   27
BLOGGING COST EQUATION (MODEL)   31
PRICING MODELS   34
THE ONE-TIME PAYMENT   35
THE UPSELL   35
THE LOAN PAYMENT MODEL   36
THE RECURRING PAYMENT MODEL   36

IT ALL COMES DOWN TO TRAFFIC -- OR DOES IT?   37

IT'S A MATTER OF CHOICES   43

IT'S YOUR BLOG, IT'S YOUR CHOICE   43
AFFILIATES, AFFILIATES EVERYWHERE AFFILIATES   44
THREE GENERIC CHOICES   45
MAKING YOUR CHOICE   46
YOUR NEXT CHOICE   47

EARNING DIRECTLY   49

WHAT IS EARNING DIRECTLY FROM YOUR BLOG   49
HOW CAN YOU EARN DIRECTLY FROM YOUR BLOG   50

EARNING DIRECTLY: SELLING ADVERTISING   55

WHAT IS THE ADVERTISING MODEL   55

HOW MUCH CAN YOU REALISTICALLY MAKE FROM ADVERTISING   57

WHERE CAN I GET ADVERTISING   58

WHAT ARE THE ADVANTAGES OF ADVERTISING   62

WHAT ARE THE DISADVANTAGES OF ADVERTISING   62

HINTS, TIPS AND GOTCHAS OF ADVERTISING   64

EARNING DIRECTLY: COMMISSION SALES   **67**

WHAT IS THE COMMISSIONS SALES MODEL   67

HOW IS COMMISSIONS SALES DIFFERENT FROM ADVERTISING   69

HOW MUCH CAN YOU REALISTICALLY MAKE FROM COMMISSION SALES   71

WHERE CAN I GET AFFILIATES   74

WHAT ARE THE ADVANTAGES OF COMMISSION SALES   77

WHAT ARE THE DISADVANTAGES OF COMMISSION SALES   78

HINTS, TIPS AND GOTCHAS OF COMMISSION SALES   81

EARNING DIRECTLY: SELLING PRODUCTS   **83**

WHAT IS THE PRODUCT SALES MODEL   83

WHAT PRODUCTS CAN I SELL   85

HOW MUCH CAN YOU REALISTICALLY MAKE FROM PRODUCT SALES   87

WHERE CAN I GET PRODUCTS   89

WHAT ARE THE ADVANTAGES OF PRODUCT SALES   90

WHAT ARE THE DISADVANTAGES OF PRODUCT SALES   91

HINTS, TIPS AND GOTCHAS OF PRODUCT SALES   92

EARNING DIRECTLY: SELLING SERVICES 95

WHAT IS THE SERVICE SALES MODEL 95

WHAT SERVICES CAN I SELL 96

HOW CAN I DELIVER SERVICES 97

HOW MUCH CAN YOU REALISTICALLY MAKE FROM SERVICE SALES 98

WHAT ARE THE ADVANTAGES OF SERVICE SALES 99

WHAT ARE THE DISADVANTAGES OF SERVICE SALES 100

HINTS, TIPS AND GOTCHAS OF SERVICE SALES 101

EARNING DIRECTLY: SELLING ACCESS 105

WHAT IS THE ACCESS SALES MODEL 105

WHAT CAN I SELL ACCESS TO 106

HOW MUCH CAN YOU REALISTICALLY MAKE FROM SELLING ACCESS 107

WHERE CAN I GET CONTENT 108

WHAT ARE THE ADVANTAGES OF SELLING ACCESS 109

WHAT ARE THE DISADVANTAGES OF SELLING ACCESS 110

HINTS, TIPS AND GOTCHAS OF SELLING ACCESS 111

EARNING INDIRECTLY 113

WHAT DO WE MEAN BY EARNING INDIRECTLY FROM YOUR BLOG? 113

EARNING INDIRECTLY: EXPERT MARKETING 117

WHAT IS EXPERT MARKETING 117

WHAT CAN I SELL WITH EXPERT MARKETING   119

HOW MUCH CAN YOU REALISTICALLY MAKE WITH EXPERT MARKETING   121

WHERE CAN I GET EXPERT MARKETING CONTENT   122

WHAT ARE THE ADVANTAGES OF EXPERT MARKETING   123

WHAT ARE THE DISADVANTAGES OF EXPERT MARKETING   124

HINTS, TIPS AND GOTCHAS OF EXPERT MARKETING   126

EARNING INDIRECTLY: SALES SUPPORT   129

WHAT IS SALES SUPPORT   129

WHAT CAN I SELL WITH SALES SUPPORT   132

WHAT PRODUCTS WORK BEST WITH SALES SUPPORT   132

HOW MUCH CAN YOU REALISTICALLY MAKE WITH SALES SUPPORT   134

WHAT ARE THE ADVANTAGES OF SALES SUPPORT   134

WHAT ARE THE DISADVANTAGES OF SALES SUPPORT   136

HINTS, TIPS AND GOTCHAS OF SALES SUPPORT   137

EARNING AROUND BLOGGING   139

WHAT IS EARNING AROUND BLOGGING?   139

EARNING AROUND BLOGGING: SELLING SERVICES   143

WHAT IS EARNING AROUND BLOGGING BY SELLING SERVICES   143

WHAT CAN I SELL AS A BLOGGING SERVICES   144

WHAT WORKS BEST AS BLOGGING SERVICES   145

How Much Can You Realistically Make with Blogging Services   146

What Are the Advantages of Selling Blogging Services   147

What Are the Disadvantages of Selling Blogging Services   149

Hints, Tips and Gotchas of Selling Blogging Services   151

EARNING AROUND BLOGGING: SELLING PRODUCTS   155

What Is Earning Around Blogging by Selling Products   155

What Can I Sell as Blogging Products   157

What Products Work Best as Blogging Products   158

How Much Can You Realistically Make with Blogging Products   159

What Are the Advantages of Selling Blogging Products   159

What Are the Disadvantages of Selling Blogging Products   161

Hints, Tips and Gotchas of Selling Blogging Products   163

CONCLUSION -- BRINGING IT ALL TOGETHER   167

Time to Make a Decision   167

Asking the Right Questions   169

Do You Already Have a Business?   169

Do You Want to Run A Business?   170

Do You Know the Technology of Your Blogging Platform Well or Can You Learn It?   170

Are You Prepared to Provide Premium Content Regularly (and Frequently)?   170

How Much Can You Realistically Make   171

ABOUT THE AUTHOR: **175**

Chapter 1:

So You Want to Be Rich

Possibilities and Promises

This is a book of possibilities. A book of dreams.

There are many reasons that guide people to blogging for money. This group of reasons can include necessity -- you are out of work and you need a source of income. Or it can include a desire to better yourself -- you are looking for a second income, or you want to stop working for someone else and work for yourself. It can include a desire to live a better life -- maybe to provide a retirement income, or an income from wherever you happen to be while you travel or a desire to live on the beach with the internet lifestyle. Or it could be as simple as a desire to have your blog pay its way.

But whatever your reasons for wanting to earn money with your blog, almost everyone who blogs reaches a point where they want their blog to earn money. Sometimes it's an epiphany, and sometimes it's an intention from the start. And sometimes, people don't even realize that's what they are doing.

Whatever the reason, blogging can help you fulfill your dreams. It can produce income for you -- from a high income to a pay-your-way income stream. It can be a source of joy and of frustration. The one thing it won't be is boring.

In this book, I'm going to share with you the information you need to make a decision. Not on if you are going to make money with your blog -- although we will discuss that. And in fact, we need to start there. But rather, we're going to focus on how you are going to turn your blog into a money machine. I'll share with you the various strategies you can use. And along the way, I'll share some of the gotchas inherent in those strategies.

Who This Book Is For

First off, let's focus on the important person. Let's start with who you are. After all, this is an advanced topic and you don't want to spend too much time on it if you aren't ready for it.

You are a new blogger. But you're not a newbie. So you already know how to blog. Maybe you've even taken a "How to Blog" course. You know the basic process. Maybe you've even done your first blog. If you haven't then don't worry -- as long as you know how to do it. In any case, you're now ready to take the next step and think about monetizing a blog. More specifically, you're ready to learn about monetizing your blog. And you're probably looking to start your first moneymaking blog.

By the way, for those of you who don't speak internet ... monetize is just a silly term that's used to indicate that you are finding a way to make money from your efforts. With the internet, there is a tendency to start companies without knowing where the money is going to come from. So this term has been coined to explain what people are doing when they figure out having an income is necessary for any company and are scrambling to avoid bankruptcy.

A Note about Income Amounts

Throughout this book, I provide estimates of the income you may be able to earn from each strategy. The purpose of these estimates is to help you understand the relative differences in income that each strategy can earn. The purpose is *not* to predict how much you will earn. These are not income projections.

Frankly, there is no way to predict how much you will earn from your blog without a personal consultation. And even then, it will be just a guess. There are just too many variables involved. One of your tasks -- if you decide to monetize your blog -- will be to monitor those variables. But without those figures, you won't be able to predict your income. And even with those ratios, you will find yourself wrong as often as you find your predictions correct.

Where possible, I've tried to base these estimates on conservative amounts. After all, I don't want you to go off believing you can get rich. That's not the point. The point is to have some way to compare potentials. And the numbers I've chosen are reasonable targets for a person new to blogging.

How This Book Is Arranged

This book is split into three major parts -- one of which is further split into two types of chapters.

The first part is the introduction to making money with a blog. Now I'm not talking about a book introduction. Rather I'm talking about a high level discussion of designing your blog's business model. And yes, your blog is a business. As soon as you start trying to make money with it, your blog becomes a business. In this section, we'll discuss some of the information you need to make rational decisions about making money with your blog. We'll also give you enough information to identify which strategies you will want to consider.

In the second part, I'll discuss the various strategies you can use to make money. This part is split into two types of chapter (and three groups -- one for each strategy group). The first chapter of a group (for example "Earning Directly") discusses the strategy group from a high level. It will discuss items which are common to all strategies in that group. The remaining chapters in the group (for example "Earning Directly: Advertising") will discuss a particular strategy in detail.

Finally, the conclusion will discuss bringing the strategies together into a single business model. Your business model.

When reading this book, I don't recommend you read the whole thing. I know, it sounds strange -- a writer recommending against reading his or her efforts. After all, this book represents a great deal of effort to write -- not to even mention the effort involved to "research" it. But nonetheless, I suggest you pick and choose what you are going to read.

I strongly recommend you read the whole of the introduction. The introduction should give you enough information to identify which of the three strategy groups interest you. However, I recommend you read only the chapters of the second part that interest you. Begin by reading the first chapter for the groups that interest you. This should give you enough information to identify which specific strategies are of interest. Then read only those chapters.

Finally, read the conclusion, which will help you to bring everything together.

If you wish, once you've read the important parts (i.e. important to you); you can go back and read the introductory chapter for the remaining strategy groups. This will give you a high-level understanding of all the strategies. And then, of course, you can go on to read anything else that interests you.

With this reading strategy, you'll get what you need out of the book, with the minimum effort on your part. Of course, it leaves me feeling unfulfilled as a writer but that's life. This book is designed to improve *your* life, not my sense of fulfillment.

Chapter 2:

Start from the Second Habit

It All Starts with Why

Now the obvious question is why is "Why?" so important? After all, it's obvious you just want to make some bucks from your blogging efforts.

The underlying thread to all of the decisions you make about your blog is the "Why?" question. Why are you blogging? Why do you want to make money with your blog? The techniques you use to make money need to be consistent with your reasons for blogging and monetizing your blog. If your why doesn't drive your decisions you'll pick the wrong method and you'll eventually stop blogging because it doesn't work or it requires too much effort.

The second reason is that your readers will know. If you aren't blogging with integrity, your readers will spot the discontinuity and they will leave. Your reasons for blogging need to flow through everything you do with respect to your blog or your readers will interpret that disconnect as a lack of integrity.

Everything we're talking about in this chapter circles around what Stephen Covey called "starting with the end in mind." You need to understand why you are doing things in order to make the right decisions to get you where you wanted to be. All your decisions are going to be driven by why you are blogging. So you want your reasons to be straightforward and easily understood.

Understanding Why

Why do you want to blog?

Why does anyone want to blog?

Everyone goes into blogging with three reasons for blogging. An outer reason, which is the reason we usually state for the blog. Maybe it's to convince others to follow our political agenda. Or maybe it's to warn others of the freemason threat and the invasion of the illuminati aliens. (Sorry, that was the silliest fringe group I could think of.) Or maybe it's to sell the advantages of writing blogs.

Whatever your outer reason, there is always another reason underlying that reason. Maybe it's compatible -- you believe in the ideals of the party, or you believe freemasons do terrible things with goats. Or maybe your underlying reason is simply that you need to make a living -- to make money. Or maybe the reason is a cause and effect relationship -- you believe in political participation, or you've been told Freemasons are non-believers or you're a blogger who wants to share his knowledge. Or maybe your underlying reason is incompatible with your outside reason -- you want to make money from the gullible. Or maybe it's unrelated and the outer reason is just a way to accomplish the inner reason and has no importance beyond that.

Underlying this second level or inner reason, there is a third reason or sub-layer. This is why you want to achieve the inner reason. Maybe you want power. Or want to keep people on the right moral path and you don't realize the source of the rumors about Freemasonry were the lies of a conman. Or you have been taught to fear what you don't understand. Or you like money and want more of it. Or you need to feed your family. It is this third layer that will truly motivate you.

And of course, your reasons can be either positive or negative.

Money vs. Ego

For our purposes, there are only two inner reasons for blogging.

You are either doing it to make money. Or you are doing it for ego reasons.

If you are doing it to make money, you need to be focused on your customer. Their needs will take precedence over yours. You'll also need to be disciplined. You're going to be running a business and you need to act like a business.

On the other hand, if you are doing it for ego reasons, you probably aren't going to be either of those. You definitely won't be focused on your readers. It's your opinion that matters. This is all about you and your beliefs and interests. And you're unlikely to be disciplined. Typically, that involves more effort than you're willing to spend.

While there really is nothing wrong with doing your blog for ego reasons, for our purposes in this course, money is the only valid inner (or second level) reason. We need for you to be disciplined. We need you to be customer driven. Going down the ego route just won't cut it.

Money as the Underlying Reason

Of course, there's always another reason behind the inner reason -- the underlying or motivating reason which we've called the third layer.

A problem arises when both reasons are the same. If you're driven strictly by money then you're probably willing to do anything to get it. And I want to stick to the positive situations here. No thieves or con men. No willingness to cheat to get ahead.

13

But there are other reasons not to do it just for money.

The first is that money alone is just a way to keep score. And it's a sliding scale. You'll never succeed if you're chasing the dollar only. Why? First, because money has no inherent value. Its only value is in what you spend it on. So it can't possibly satisfy or motivate long term. And secondly, because the definition of enough money becomes a moving target. No matter how much you earn you'll always want more. And if you can never reach your emotional goals, you'll soon lose motivation.

The second reason is that once we achieve a basic level of survival, money is no longer a motivator. It sounds silly, but it's true. What motivates us after that, are the things that money can buy us. Time, social acceptance, family life, personal growth and so on. When we see money as the motivator, we're really just taking the easy way out and not bothering to look for what is really motivating us.

Well if money isn't acceptable, what else could be a strong motivator?

The answer is that it's strictly up to you. Your motivating reason can be anything at all. From spending more time with your family, to a bigger house, to time for study, to building your professional reputation. It can be finding a job. It can be selling lots of widgets.

It is strictly personal. Your motivating reason can be a short term or a long-term goal. It can be an intermediate or an ultimate goal.

In fact, it's probably going to be a mix of long term and short term, intermediate and ultimate goals. But whatever your motivating reason is, your reason and my reason aren't going to be the same. And the person beside you is going to be different as well. Your kids will have different reasons. Your spouse will have different reasons. The reason will be as unique as you are.

So you need to figure it out for yourself.

No one else can. All anyone else can do is to help you in the search. All we can do is help *you* find the answer.

The Effects of Why

But whatever the reasons and the relationship between those reasons, why you are blogging has four major effects:

1. It's going to affect the discipline that you bring to your blogging efforts. It's going to affect how you view the discipline necessary for blogging efficiently.
2. It's going to affect the morality of your blogging efforts. Of course, your own moral code is also going to put limits on what you are willing to do.
3. It's going to affect who you are focused on. Is it yourself? Or your reader?
4. For our purposes, your motivations are being described by the reasons. This is what is going to keep you going when it gets hard. This is what is going to get you up in the morning.

If you are writing a blog for money, you need to be very disciplined with your blog. You need to treat it as a business. That means you need to produce a blog entry on a regular basis. It can't be sometimes, then sometimes not. Maybe I'll do it today. Maybe I won't. It has to be out on every Monday, every Tuesday, or once a week or once a month. Or whatever schedule you choose. It doesn't really matter what the schedule is. What matters is that it is regular and that your customers can expect it.

If you are writing for personal reasons, it really doesn't matter. You put out a blog entry whenever you feel like it. Quality can be whatever you feel like on any particular day.

You also need to think about it from the viewpoint of driving traffic. If you are writing a blog to make money, you need to be disciplined in your traffic efforts. If you are doing it for personal reasons, you can just let the blog sit there and not do anything for traffic. It may not be the smartest thing to do but it certainly is possible.

The next issue is morality. Let's face it. If you are blogging for business purposes, you have to be on the up and up. You need to be honest or your customers will never buy from you again. And most governments have some form of enforcement to ensure business does not rip-off their customers.

Blogging for personal reasons? Well, okay. Personally, I require everything I do to be on the up and up. I'm just not

17

going to be dishonest. But, if you're doing it for personal reasons theoretically your own moral code has to direct you. And even then you could ignore your basic moral code (unlikely but you could). In business, there is too much going on around you. You can't afford to go over the edge of the border between honesty and dishonesty. You will get caught.

Then there is your focus. In a business or moneymaking blog, you have to focus on your customer. Your reader -- who is your customer -- has to be at the forefront of your mind at all times. You have to put yourself in their shoes whenever you are doing anything. Whenever you are looking at things, you have to see it from their point of view. Your own point of view is sitting there, but it's in the background. It's the inner reason. Your outer reason has to be very clear and it has to be their reason not yours.

For a personal blog, it doesn't matter. Your focus is automatically on what you're blogging for. And if your reader is along for the ride then cool. In simple terms, when it's a personal blog, it just plain doesn't matter if the readers like it.

Finally, blogging isn't a sprint. It's a marathon. And as everyone knows, you need to be motivated to finish a marathon. If you aren't motivated, you won't even finish getting your blog set up. If you are motivated then you will succeed in making money with your blog. And other blogs as well. It all comes down to having the knowledge and being motivated enough to apply that knowledge despite the effort.

But motivating yourself isn't quite the same as motivating someone else. Most of the rules are essentially the same. The same things will motivate you that would motivate others. However, how you do it and the rules governing how you do it change. When motivating yourself, you need to be very clear, and upfront with your reasoning. When motivating someone else you'll need to try different tactics and you might apply the motivations occasionally. You are guessing and your methods need to take that into account. However, when motivating yourself not only do you need to know exactly what your motivation is, but you also need to be constantly reminded of those reasons.

Getting to Why

Okay, so now it's time to get down to brass tacks. What you have to do is identify why you want to blog and why you want to make money with your blog. You need to identify both the inner and outer reasons for you to blog and make money with your blog. More importantly, you need to identify the third level or underlying reasons for blogging. These reasons will form your motivation. You can stop now and do that or you can continue with the next chapter. However, you do need to identify your reasons before you can consider this book complete. You need to know why before you make any decision on how you will make money with your blog.

So what's the best way to identify your reasons?

Start by grabbing a pencil and several pieces of paper. An eraser is also a good idea, although you may want to scratch out instead of erasing. Then find yourself a quiet area where you can work without any interruptions.

Your first piece of paper is going to be your readers' view. Start by putting the outer reason at the top of the page. This is the reason behind your blog. It's why your reader comes to your blog. Then describe your typical reader. Who are they? What is their name? Are they married? Single? Do they have kids? How old are they? What do they do for a living? What do they do for fun? Write down anything and everything that you can think of about them. Use several pieces of paper if you have to. This typical reader will become your target reader. Next, write down how you can connect with them. Do they hang out at certain blogs or forums? Do they read certain e-zines? Finally, list out the problems or issues about your topic that would most interest your typical reader.

Now it's time to move your view from your reader to yourself. Begin with a fresh piece of paper. At the top, write down why you are writing your blog. Don't overthink it. If you're having problems expressing your reasons start by stating your first reason as either money or ego. There was a reason we simplified into only two reasons. Start from that simplification and then build out to more detail. Use point form to list your reasons. Under that list of reasons, draw three columns. In the first column, write down areas in your current life that you feel are important. In the second column, write down how your life is now in that area. In the third column, write down how your life will be different when you become successful with your blog. Finally, summarize your third layer (i.e. motivating or underlying) reasons.

If you have problems identifying the important areas of your life, then try a slightly different tack. Start with your outer reason(s). Then ask "Why?" five times. This will give you a good way of pushing through to the root cause of your desires. However, you may find that the information you gain isn't complete. In that case, consider doing the three-column exercise after asking your fifth "Why?" question.

Chapter 3:

Models, Money and Mayhem

What is a Model and Why Should I Care?

What is the difference between a model and theory?

Complexity is a fact of real life. One of the biggest problems facing modern man is simply cutting through the extraneous garbage until you're able to see what is really happening. This is sometimes referred to as cutting something down to the bone. For example, writing to the bone or drawing to the bone or blogging to the bone. Of course, once you've gotten rid of the chaff, the next problem is to make sense of what remains.

Theory and models are two ways to do that. Theory does it by asking, "Why?" Why does an apple fall to the earth? Why does an atomic bomb explode? It seeks to understand the underlying causes of an observed situation. A model on the other hand is much more prosaic. It asks the question "What?" What happens when I drop two objects? What happens in an atomic bomb? Models seek to record knowledge about the situation in a manner that is understandable and useable.

Models can be used to observe and record what is happening. For example, there is a communications model describing what is happening when two people talk. But models can also be used to plan or describe a plan. An architectural drawing is a type of model. So is an architectural model (the three dimensional kind).

Businesses (including a blog) are complex systems. And they vary. Every business is unique. Even if two businesses are in the same industry, they have characteristics that distinguish them, one from the other. And because they are unique and complex, describing them as a group is an exercise in futility.

This is where models come in. Models describe complex classes of systems in simple terms. They focus on only what is important.

There are several models that are of importance in any business. For example, your business model describes how you will make money. Your profit model describes how you will translate sales into profits. Your sales funnel is a model that describes the stages your customer will go through as they move from attention to your message to the purchase of your product. These models allow you to describe your plan for your business in understandable chunks.

And blogging for money is a business. It too has models.

There are five models that are of importance to you and I as we work through this book:

1. The strategic model
2. The sales process model
3. The sales funnel model
4. The cost model
5. The pricing model

The strategic model describes your business and the strategies it will use to make money. Effectively, it is the whole purpose of this book. We'll address it in the next chapter, and in the following chapters.

The sales process model describes the steps that a business needs to go through in order to sell their product. Effectively it describes how the business will transform a lead into a sale. We will examine a very high level (and somewhat simplified) version of this model for internet based sales in a moment.

The sales funnel describes the stages a customer moves through as they move from awareness of your product (or before) to purchase. It deals with the same area of concern as the sales process model. However, it looks at it from the viewpoint of the customer's movement rather than the tasks the company goes through. Although this model is important to you, there are many variations. In fact, it is unique to your business. I'm going to leave it to you to determine your own sales funnel.

The cost model describes where you will be spending the money that the sales process brings in. In effect, it will describe how you spend money to produce whatever it is you sell. We'll examine a generic version associated with internet businesses later in this chapter.

Finally, the pricing model describes the various methods of pricing. In this chapter, we'll examine the various techniques you can use to price your product. However, how you actually combine those methods is part of your planning process. It is one of the decisions you'll need to make as part of your strategic model. So we'll focus here on presenting generic models.

Sales Models and Processes

Which sort of leads us into the typical blog's business model and the parts we need to make sales work. There are three basic sales process models that apply to internet sales (including blogging):

1. The catch-as-catch-can model
2. The advertising model
3. The ongoing contact model

The first two sales process models can be considered as variations on the last one. Effectively the catch-as-catch-can and advertising models consist of not bothering to perform certain actions in the ongoing contact model. While they can be viable models on their own, generally they are less effective than the ongoing contact or networking model. So we're going to focus on explaining only the ongoing contact model.

The ongoing contact model consists of three parts:

1. Traffic creation
2. Opt-in
3. Contact maintenance

It all starts with the blog getting traffic -- in other words visitors to your blog who actually look at one or more webpages. That traffic can be from anywhere. In our other books and courses, we give you the knowledge and tools to use your blog's content to generate traffic. For that matter so does every other internet marketer who teaches about building a business on the internet. So I'm not going to go into the how here. But somehow, you attract traffic to the blog.

The more traffic your website gets, the more advertising clicks your readers make. You may have ads on your blog from Google and others but you also have your own ads. In any case, the more traffic, the more likely your blog readers are to click somewhere important.

Within your site, one of the first clicks is going to be your opt-in page. This is usually some form of ethical bribe. Either a free eBook or a free report or a free course. Something that will induce your customer to give you their name and email address in exchange for your product. Just to clarify here, theoretically it's not free. It just costs the customer their permission rather than a dollar amount.

What your customer has given their permission for (called opting-in) is to receive an email campaign. This is your ongoing contact. It can be in the form of an email or in the form of a newsletter. However, it must be consistent, relevant and personalized. So you're going to be sending them an email -- targeted to their needs -- every few days.

This technique is sometimes called email marketing. However, it is just as frequently called relationship marketing. And while email marketing describes the tool used, relationship marketing is perhaps a better description. After all, the whole purpose behind the emails is to establish a relationship with your customers. Through that relationship, you can build trust, identify issues, build interest in your blog and ultimately sell them your products.

Finally, your email campaign sends customers to your sales page. This finalizes the sale and acts as the beginning of the order entry process. Of course, in the real world (rather than the model), the emails continue and the customer is directed to a sales page until the campaign runs out.

Now, time for a quick clarification. Email marketing is not spamming. Spamming is spamming no matter what the form. It doesn't have to be in email form. In fact, if your blog invites comments you are going to attract spammers. Spamming is imposing your marketing message on people who do not want to see it. It can be done with email. It can be done with blog comments. It can be done with websites that promise information and provide a sales message instead.

What we're talking about is sending information only to people who have knowingly asked for the information. This is known as permission based or opt-in marketing. The more above board you are, the better. That means a clear and easy opt-out process. It means a double opt-in process where the first email is a request for confirmation of the customer's permission. And it means a very clear notice that you will be sending them sales letters.

So given the ongoing contact model as our generic model, let's look at where the costs for a blog come in ....

Blogging Cost Equation (Model)

First off, remember that everything costs -- either time and energy or money. If you do it yourself, it's costing you time and energy. If you outsource it, it costs you money. The question just becomes -- what is your time worth? And how much can you afford?

So what does it cost to run a blog?

There are four basic costs:

1. Cost of traffic
2. Cost of content

3. Product costs
4. Overhead costs

The first is the cost of obtaining traffic. You could take out an AdWords campaign. That'll cost you per click. Or you could optimize your site in order to get free traffic. That'll cost you time and energy or if you give it to someone else it'll cost you money. Fairly big money. You could use content marketing or its splinter, article marketing. Again if you do it yourself it will cost you time and energy. If you give it to someone else, it'll cost you money.

The next cost is that of the content. After all, a blog without anything in it isn't much of a blog. In our other courses, we show you how to get the most out of your blog content. In any case, creating content is going to cost you to produce it. And quality content is going to cost more than the simpler content used to generate traffic.

However, our generic business model was built around product sales and advertising. So we need to consider the cost of producing the products. For the opt-in product if nothing else. Terminology is going to change based on the actual product chosen. And to a certain extent, the number of segments we break the cost into might change. But no matter how you cut it, you have a cost associated with designing the product, building the product and distributing the product.

Finally, you have a number of overhead costs. We've called them hosting. But it's the cost of keeping your site up and it includes a number of costs. It isn't very much -- probably under $200 per year. Things like your ISP's hosting program and your domain registration are examples of these costs.

There are two bottom lines to this discussion.

The first is that traffic and sales are proportional. More traffic means more sales. Less traffic means fewer sales.

And second, is that while there are several methods to obtain traffic or product, there is a cost associated with all the methods. And your costs need to be lower than your price if you want to make money.

Pricing Models

In a generic form, pricing models describe how the individual sale becomes total income. Typically, the model will include how the cost and the price are related. However, for our purposes, we're only going to look at the income side. More specifically the method used to price the product. Of course, this only applies to product and service sales. Other income models such as commissions and advertising will be dealt with in their appropriate chapters.

When it comes to pricing, the internet is a bit of a free-for-all. As much as its Wild, Wild West nature has calmed since the dot-bomb era, it still tends to show the characteristics of an immature market. That includes the fact that pricing models have not settled into a single form yet. Typically, in a mature market there would be only one or two pricing models in use (at least as far as we are defining pricing model). However, in internet sales -- even within single markets -- there are at least four basic pricing models in use:

1. The one-time payment
2. The upsell

3. The loan payment
4. The recurring payment

The One-Time Payment

The one-time payment is the typical retail store pricing model. You know, the one you see every time you go into the grocery store or a department store. You have one price for the product where the total product sales times the price must be greater than all the costs associated with the product. This is also sometimes referred to as a unit cost or single unit cost. Over the internet most of these prices end in 7 based on advice from Dan Kennedy. For example, the most common price points are $7, $17, $27, $47, $97, $127, $147, $197, $297, $497, $597, $997, $1997 and $2997.

The Upsell

In theory, this shouldn't be a pricing model. However, on the internet it is. It is based on the McDonald's "Would you like fries with that?" sales technique. Essentially, you are looking to sell a package of products. The initial one is low priced and possibly even a (legal) loss leader. When the buyer commits to buying that product, you begin a series of related offers in the hopes that they will buy more products. Typically, these offers represent a one-time savings over the individual price.

The Loan Payment Model

Two of the problems that you will run into when selling high-ticket items, are a lack of trust and an inability to pay. A solution to both those issues is the loan payment model. With this model, you take the one-time price and spread it over a series of payments. So for example, a $997 product could be paid in three installments of $337. You'll notice that the total of the monthly payments ($1011) is higher than the original price. This is typical for this form of payment schedule. Normally this is blamed on interest, but is usually more a matter of rounding to the next $7 than true interest.

The Recurring Payment Model

How hard is it to sell a $197 product? How hard is it to sell a $19.97 product? Big difference, isn't it? That's the basis of the recurring payment model. The concept is that rather than sell a single product for a single (or series of) billings, you sell the same product over a series of months. For example, you could sell a four-hour DVD course for $197. This would represent a great deal of work (roughly 160 hours or 1 month). And the chances of selling it would be low. Or you could break the course into 12 modules of 20 minutes each. Then sell access to the module on a monthly payment of $19.97. Each 20-minute module would represent about 8 hours of work per month. The chances of selling your product is much higher and if the average customer stays for 10 months, you will earn the full sale. If they stay for the full course (12 months), you'll earn an extra 20%. Not only that, but some customers will stay on past the 12 months resulting in further product sales.

It All Comes Down to Traffic -- Or Does It?

As we've worked our way through the thought process of making money with your blog, we've mentioned repeatedly the concept of traffic. If you get more traffic, you get more sales. That's basic sales theory. It's a numbers game.

But that's only part of the story.

There are several types of traffic. Some will be of use to you. Some will be a problem for you. Some may produce a few bucks to offset their costs. Some won't. The key is to produce as much traffic that pays you as you can. If you don't earn from the traffic it isn't valuable and in fact, you'd rather not have it. Remember that, as we said earlier, everything costs either money or time. With the wrong traffic, you'll pay twice. Once to get the traffic. And once to service the traffic. Remember that most ISPs cap your traffic -- they put an upper limit on your included traffic. You pay extra for anything above that limit.

So let's start by looking at raw traffic. This is the amount of traffic that is looking for whatever your blog is about. The easiest way to estimate that is to look at the keywords for your blog and then check Google's AdWords Keyword Tool. You can find this tool by searching Google for "adwords keyword". Bing also has a webmaster tool that includes the equivalent search analysis tool. However, since Google accounts for 64% of all searches on the web, it makes sense to use their tool. An alternative is to use a keyword analyzer or aggregator such as nichebot.com. These tools combine searches from the major search firms and add a number of analysis tools.

Of course, no matter how much raw search traffic you might get, you will only receive a portion of that traffic. The amount you actually get will depend on a number of factors. Most especially the amount of traffic that you are generating through alternatives to search, and your position in the search. Such factors as keyword frequency and link popularity will affect how near the first page in the search you get, and thus the amount of search traffic you get. But even with a strong search optimization strategy, only a certain number of searchers will click through to your website.

The number of people who actually click through to your website is your first click-through rate or CTR. The CTR is a simple calculation used throughout the internet sales process. It is simply the number of clicks divided by the amount of traffic. It's usually expressed as a percentage. Effectively, it measures the amount of traffic that is passing that stage of the sales funnel.

Which click-through rates (CTRs) matter to you will depend on your definition of a sales funnel. For example, let's take the example from article marketing. You have a funnel which consists of the following stages:

1. Search requested
2. Search displayed
3. Article read
4. Blog read
5. Opt-in page read
6. Emails sent
7. Emails read
8. Product page read
9. Product purchased

Each of the first eight stages will have an associated click-through rate. Your customer will need to search for your keyword. Google will then need to include your listing on the page. Your customer will need to click on the search return in order to see the article. They will then need to click on the link at the end of the article to view your blog. They then need to click on your ad or link to visit your opt-in page. And so on through each stage of the funnel. Of course, once they have purchased the product, they are no longer in the funnel. So theoretically, there is no click at that point.

Of course, not all these stages are important. For example, the first two stages (search requested and displayed) are often ignored. Although Google Webmaster Tools (and now Google Analytics) do provide this information.

One of the decisions you'll need to make is which click-through rates (and by extension which traffic quantities) are important to you. And which ones are not.

So why are these click-through rates so important?

The obvious answer is that your efforts are being judged and the click-through rate is the measure of that judgment. The better your CTRs, the better you have done. If you improve your quality at each stage, your CTR will improve. However, it isn't that simple.

Each market is different. Not only are you measuring your ability to convert a visitor at that stage to a visitor at the next stage, but you are also measuring the market's willingness to take that step. For example, the average CTR for articles published on EzineArticles is around 7%. My writing articles produce slightly more than that number. However, my project management articles produce a lowly 2%. My blogging articles produce 25% or better. Even though all of the articles are written by the same person and to the same level of quality. The difference is partially the reactivity or responsiveness of each of those micro-markets. And, in part, the difference is where you are publishing. My articles, which are republished on other project management blogs, have a click-through of plus 25%. These are literally the same article picked up from EzineArticles but with vastly different CTRs. The only difference is where they are found.

Chapter 4:

It's a Matter of Choices

It's Your Blog, It's Your Choice

Okay, so we know our motivation. We know why monetizing our blog is important to us. We know what will motivate us to do the work involved in blogging. We know the underlying direction for all our decisions. We've looked at the different models that we need to identify and develop. We've even discussed the importance of traffic and some of the analytics we will need to track. It's time to go on and look at the ways we can earn money from our blog. We'll start by looking at it from a high level.

But first, I need to clarify a problem with terminology.

Affiliates, Affiliates Everywhere Affiliates

English speakers are a lazy bunch when it comes to language. We reuse and duplicate and misuse and abuse our terminology all the time. That means you need to clarify exactly what is meant when you hear a term out in the real world. In this book, I'm going to be as careful as I can, but people change meanings all the time.

Let me give you an example.

If I use the word affiliate, you need to ask me what is meant. Why? Because it has several meanings. And how you are using it at any point in time will vary considerably.

For example, I can use the term affiliate to refer to people who sell my products. I can also use the term to refer to people whose products I sell. I can be paid for those products in the form of a small commission or a large commission. I can also co-sell products where my affiliate does a mailing selling my products and I do a mailing selling his or hers. All of these are called affiliate marketing. But they are entirely different models.

In fact, I used affiliate as an example here because it can be a direct earnings technique, an indirect technique or a technique that's not even on the moneymaking board -- all depending on how and where it is used and more importantly, what we're talking about at the time. I'm therefore going to avoid using affiliate marketing as a description of an earnings technique. I will however, occasionally refer to affiliate marketing as an example of a strategy.

Three Generic Choices

There are three basic strategies for monetizing or earning money from a blog. They are:

1. Direct
2. Indirect
3. Around blogging

You can earn money directly from your blog. Your blog is actually producing income. And it exists for the purposes of producing income.

The second strategy is indirect. Your blog is actually a marketing expense. It exists to drive customers to your existing business. So you make money from somewhere else.

And the third strategy is making money around blogging. Essentially, you earn by selling your expertise about blogging in the form of either products or services. Your blog's subject really doesn't matter. It's blogging in general that matters.

Making Your Choice

Now let's stop here for a second.

In this book, I'm going to treat each of these strategies as single, standalone alternatives. They aren't.

In the real world, you are going to want to mix and match. You're going to pick two, three, four or whatever number of detailed strategies or techniques and use them to make money. Whatever makes sense to you. Chances are they will be from different generic or base strategies. That's cool. The mix of strategies is part of what defines your business. It's your business model. It's your choice.

46

Your Next Choice

You are now ready to go on and read the second part of the book. Before you start, make a decision on which strategies you want to learn more about. Or perhaps, I should say which strategies you may want to apply.

There are three sets of chapters in the following section, one for each of the three generic strategies:

1. Earning Directly
2. Earning Indirectly
3. Earning around blogging

Each set of chapters has an introduction chapter. Read the introductory chapters that are of most interest to you. This will give you a better understanding of the alternatives within each generic strategy. From there you can decide which strategies interest you. Then read only the chapters of interest.

And of course, in the conclusion, I'll bring everything together and give you some further hints about making your choices.

Chapter 5:

Earning Directly

What is Earning Directly From Your Blog

Okay, so now that we know why we're blogging and the three generic strategies, let's start looking closer at the possibilities. An obvious place to start is with making money from the blog itself. We call that directly monetizing your blog.

One of the most common ways to make money over the internet is with content. Content is information formatted in a useful way. Your blog is just another form of content. So are videos, podcasts, articles, webinars and courses.

Content can also be used to create traffic. (Okay, content can't create traffic per se. Content draws interested people to it. For the sake of brevity, we call that creating traffic). That traffic can be utilized in several ways to make money.

The obvious first strategy, is to make money directly from the blog. The blog pays for itself by selling something it has. This can be either the content within the blog or the traffic it generates. Selling traffic typically involves either redirecting the attention of the readers within the site or to other sites.

How Can You Earn Directly From Your Blog

There are five major ways to make money with your blog. We'll cover each of them in detail in a moment. Right now, I want to summarize them.

You can monetize your blog directly by:

1. Selling advertising
2. Commission sales (which is one form that affiliate sales takes)

3. Selling a product
4. Selling a service
5. Selling access

Selling advertising on your blog is the same as selling advertising for a paper-based newspaper or magazine. You allocate space on your blog for someone else to advertise on and then sell it. For most of us, that means using an ad clearinghouse of some kind. Payment may be based on rotations (also called impressions) or you may be paid only when your reader clicks on the advertisement.

You can also do commission sales. This is typically referred to as affiliate sales (or at least one variation) or as payment on action. With advertising, you get paid a small amount either for the ad placement or for someone clicking on the ad. In commission sales, you don't make anything until something is actually sold (or at least until the reader takes an action on the advertiser's site).

You can also sell a product on your blog. This is probably the most common method of making money with your blog. Products can be either physical or virtual. That is they can exist in the real world -- and be touched, shipped etc.. Or they can exist as recordings in the computer. In fact, you probably bought this book over the internet in the Kindle edition. Although Amazon and its competitors are not blogs, this is essentially the same process we are talking about when we use the term virtual. If you've bought the paperback version, then you've bought the physical version.

You can sell a service on your blog. This is essentially the same thing as selling a product. The only difference is that we're talking about a service and not a product. These services can be delivered on-site or remotely. Coaching is probably the most common form that this type of service takes. However, many other types of services (e.g. web design and mobile app coding) can be sold this way.

Finally, you can sell access. This is really just a specialized form of product. In this case, what you're really selling is access to something. Unlike a product, which may be a recurring payment but usually is a one-time payment; this is almost always a recurring payment. As long as the payment is current, the access continues. Recurring payments have some major advantages as we discussed in the recurring payment pricing model in chapter 3.

In the following chapters we'll get into the details behind these strategies and talk about some of the benefits and disadvantages of each.

Chapter 6:

Earning Directly: Selling Advertising

What Is the Advertising Model

Advertising is probably the most common method used to make money from a blog. It's basically a set and forget type solution. As long as you're driving traffic, you should be able to make money from the ads. It doesn't require you to do anything once you've put the ad on the site.

Advertising on a blog is basically the same model as newspapers and magazines have used for years. Centuries now, I guess. With a slight twist based on the interactive nature of the internet. The interactive nature of the internet means that we aren't locked into selling ads using a flat price based on the size of the ad and an estimate of the amount of traffic. Instead, we can base the price on sizes and actual responses in the form of the number of times displayed or in the form of reader activity.

There are two very basic payment models. The first is banner advertising where you are paid based on the number of impressions. An impression or rotation is the number of times the ad is seen by a reader. This is almost the magazine model. Size times impressions times rate gives the amount paid. The more times your ad is seen the more you get paid. The more space the more you earn. The only difference is that on the internet if someone doesn't look at the ad you don't get paid. In a magazine, the presumption is that if it's in the magazine it will be seen by the readers.

The second advertising payment model is based on the viewer taking an action. In that model, you get paid not on impressions and size but on size and the number of times your readers click on the ad. When the reader clicks on the ad they are connected to the advertiser's site. So effectively, you are being paid to drive traffic to your advertiser's site.

And of course, there are those advertising networks or advertisers who try to play both sides and do a mix of the two models.

The problem for you as a blogger, of course, is that many of the advertising companies charge their customers using the impressions model and they pay you on a click basis. This puts all the risk of readers not clicking on both you the blogger and on their customer the actual advertiser. Of course, the advertising network avoids any risk and uses that lack of risk to boost their own profits. What this means to you is that if you are advertising to drive traffic, you have to be very careful to know and understand exactly what you are being charged for and what your click through and conversion rates are. Otherwise, you could find yourself spending more to drive traffic to your site than your site is making.

How Much Can You Realistically Make from Advertising

Determining how much your site can make from advertising can be an exercise in frustration. However, for a typical site with 1000 visitors and 2000 page views per month you can make roughly $5.00 to $20.00 per month. Not a great deal but it can add up over time. And especially if you have multiple blogs.

You can improve this number in four ways:

1. Increase the traffic
2. Have a highly responsive clientele
3. Increase the number of advertisements on the page
4. Increase the number of advertisements above the fold.

Where Can I Get Advertising

Which sort of leads to the next bit of information.

There are five main sources of advertising available:

1. Google AdSense
2. Ad rotators
3. Managed affiliates

4. Self-managed affiliates
5. True affiliate partners

The first major source of advertising is Google Adsense. They are fairly powerful and ubiquitous. In many ways, they own the market. They pay once a month. However, you need to have $100 owed to you for them to cut a check. They also charge you for paying by check if you are in the US. So it is best if you have them make direct deposits to a US bank account.

Google, by the way, is one of the few search engines that spreads the joy. Most of the other search engines only sell advertising for their own site. Google allows you to buy advertising (through their AdWords product) which they then provide through to yourself and others as AdSense. So when you buy an AdWords ad, they will display it to any AdSense customer they choose. You do have some control as an AdSense publisher to exclude competitors but Google makes most of the decisions over what will and won't show on your site. While there is some focus on your site and the information you have, most of the targeting of the ads is based on the interests of the reader. This helps to increase the response rates to the ads. However, it also means that everyone who uses AdSense is displaying the same ads to a reader. The reader may click now or later. Your blog has little influence on when or if the reader clicks. So there is a certain amount of randomness to when a reader clicks.

The next source for advertising is the banner advertisers or ad rotators. These vary from good to bad. As a group, they do have a reputation for not vetting their advertisers. In other words, rotators routinely end up serving viruses and so forth. Ad rotators also have a habit of committing privacy violations from their own actions as well. Unfortunately, tracking your habits as a web viewer can easily lead to tracking all your habits or to using questionable methods of obtaining more information. Technically, Google is an ad rotator. The only reason Google isn't part of this group is its sheer size and importance.

The next source for advertising is managed affiliates. These are companies such as Amazon or Barnes & Noble that have affiliate programs managed by an ad rotator service. These services often call themselves affiliate management services but they will frequently approach you to add other affiliates to your site. For our purposes, there is little or no difference between an affiliate management service and an ad rotator.

Amazon is actually a bad example of a managed affiliate. It really is a self-managed affiliate. Self-managed affiliates are companies with a predesigned affiliate program just like a managed affiliate. You either accept their rules and payments or you don't act as an affiliate. However in this case, the self-managed affiliate manages their affiliate program rather than using an ad rotator to handle payments and so on. As a result, you will only be serving ads from them. And the self-managed affiliate won't be constantly bugging you to carry someone else's ads.

Up to this point, we've been describing companies where you sign up with their pre-designed affiliate program.

Another option is the true affiliate partner. These are sites that you have negotiated an ad exchange with directly. They may have a standardized affiliate program, but typically becoming an affiliate is not as easy as it is with the automated companies. And you are sometimes able to negotiate the actual commissions being paid. Email swaps and other mutual advertising techniques are often side benefits of this type of arrangement. (If you haven't heard the term before, an email swap is where you mail the other person's offer to your customers. In return the other person mails your offer to their customers.).

What Are the Advantages of Advertising

The big advantage of using advertising is that it is a "set and leave" system. Once you set it up and add the code to the site, it just runs in the background. As long as you are getting the traffic, you will be getting an income.

You can use advertising anywhere. It's the ubiquitous moneymaker. It just sits there and brings in the cash. However, depending on why you are blogging, you may want the ads to be less or more subtle. If your main purpose for your blog is selling your own products, then having someone else's ad may be counter-productive. Remember that the ads may actually be for your competitors.

What Are the Disadvantages of Advertising

The big downside for advertising is the low income potential. Your average blog probably isn't producing much more than $10 to $200 per month in advertising revenues.

Traffic is the main predictor so it is possible to earn more but it's also very unlikely.

A second downside of advertising on your blog is that clicking on an ad will usually cause your reader to leave your site. Not only does this mean you lose any further sales but it also means that you won't know which of your readers is actually buying from the people you are advertising for.

Third, you have no real control on which ads are showing up on your site. You could easily find yourself advertising your competitors' products. Although many ad rotators have tools that allow you to select which ads to avoid, it is most likely that some competitors will end up advertising on your site.

A fourth issue is the fact that you have to wait to be paid. Most companies will only pay you if you are over a certain limit (usually $100). In fact, some also charge you fees on top. So unless you are driving sufficient traffic to generate high fees, you may actually never be paid anything. The only person who gets rich is the ad rotator who pockets the unpaid revenues.

Finally, advertising rotators (including Google) are involved in virus distribution via the web. Presumably without their knowledge. However, all it takes is for virus kiddies to sign on to the ad site, pay the fee and then upload a Trojan or virus stream. The ad site takes care of the rest and happily distributes the virus to everyone who visits a site that is displaying ads from that carrier. And if you happen to be carrying that ad, you are going to be happily distributing that malware to all your visitors. Which means you'll get the blame.

Hints, Tips and Gotchas of Advertising

Now there are a couple of hints and unique characteristics to keep in mind when considering advertising as a monetization scheme.

First off, where you place the ad matters a great deal. If you are being paid on impressions -- that is by the number of people seeing the ad, -- then you definitely want to place the ad as high in the web page as possible. There is a concept called "above the fold" in web design. The fold is that point where the first screen stops. In other words, if your ad is "above the fold" it will show to every viewer. If it's below the fold, it will only show to those who chose to scroll down the page.

This is important even if you aren't being paid on impressions. The more impressions you get the higher your number of clicks and the more you'll be paid. So you want to keep most of your ads above the fold. Because if an ad isn't seen, then it can't be clicked on.

However, in some cases, you're going to want to put an ad in a specific place within the content. In this case, you are using the content itself to sell the product. The ad is just a call to action. It's a way to jump to the sales page. In that case, you want to place the ad in the position where you think most people will be most convinced to click. That can be a little difficult to predict but you get the idea. Often these specifically placed ads are repeated throughout the blog page.

On the other hand, you don't want to become an advertising rag. Too many ads will lower the perception of quality your blog needs. Effectively, your blog will become the equivalent of an opportunities or sales magazine. These magazines really exist to distribute advertisements and their articles tend to be "fluff" pieces. On the internet, a reputation of publishing pure "fluff" can result in your blog dying a slow and painful death.

Chapter 7:

Earning Directly: Commission Sales

What Is the Commissions Sales Model

Somewhere between advertising and selling your own products or services is the concept called commission sales. This is where you advertise on your blog and drive traffic to someone else's blog. In return, you get a percentage of any sales made to that customer. It really is a matter of receiving commissions on any sales that occur with a customer you have driven to the seller's site.

Advertising and Commission sales are often the first two techniques used by new bloggers. They are both easy to set up and use. They both require little if any maintenance.

And the only real difference is the method of determining how much you will be paid. With advertising, it is calculated with an action occurring on your site. With commission sales, it is based on an action on your advertiser's site.

There are two basic methods for making money with commissions.

The first is usually called affiliate marketing. But then again almost everything is called affiliate marketing. Unlike affiliate marketing under the advertising banner, payment is made based on any sales over a certain period. However, the driving force for income is the display ad. Exactly the same as in advertising. In fact, many affiliates require you to sell only through display ads and will cancel your account if they find you are using email or alternative marketing. They do this because they wish to preserve their brand from damage by spammers.

There is also another version of commission affiliate sales. This tends to be with smaller companies and involves directly arranging to co-sell or sell their products. You can sell their products through ads in your blog, through actual sales letters or through mentioning it in your email marketing.

Frequently this is set up on an individual basis so you have a great deal of flexibility. Some companies will set up a variety of tools to support their preferred methods. Clickbank products are a good example of this type of commission sales.

How Is Commissions Sales Different from Advertising

Advertising and commission based selling are almost the same. They both use the same display ad tools. And in fact, typically, you don't discover which form you are getting involved in until you investigate and sign up for a company's affiliate program. It could be advertising or it could be commissions. Or they could have both and let you pick one or the other or both.

The first principal difference is the method of determining payment. With advertising, you are limited to some form of action in the current session on your site. This could be displaying the ad (called an impression or rotation) or clicking on the ad. With a commission-based payment scheme, nothing is paid until a purchase is made on your advertiser's site. Occasionally, payment is based on another action (such as your reader opting into their email campaigns). However, a sale is by far the most common action triggering a commission payment.

The second principal difference is the period being covered. With an advertisement based system, the earning potential is restricted to the current session. After all, the payment is based on either the ad being shown or the reader clicking on the ad. But, whichever it is, earning occurs in real time. With a commission sale, that isn't necessarily true. Sales could occur months or even years after providing the lead. So the commissions are paid for any sales in a defined period. This period could be limited to just the current session or it could be 30, 60 or 90 days or in some cases, even longer. In fact, some affiliates pay commissions on all purchases from that customer as long as they are a customer of the affiliate.

The third principal difference is how the payment is calculated. With advertising, the payment amount is always consistent. There may be rules and groups of payments but the payment is a flat amount. As for the commission, it could be based on a percentage or on a flat amount. For example, some affiliates will pay for people signing up to their opt-in page. And of course, that involves a flat fee per lead. On the other hand, others pay based on a percentage of the total sales to the customer over the period.

The fourth principal difference is in the amount of the payment. With advertising, the rate is always a small amount. After all, there is no guarantee that the customer will actually spend money with the advertiser. So the payment rate is always a low amount, usually between $0.10 and $2.00 although rates of less than one cent and more than five dollars do occur.

On the other hand, commission based sales pay much higher rates on much lower activities. Fifty percent rates are not unheard of. For example, selling a $997 product for someone else could easily net you $485. This is how the major gurus make most of their money -- commissions from selling someone else's products.

How Much Can You Realistically Make from Commission Sales

As hard as it is to estimate the income from advertising, it is even harder to guess at the income possible from commission sales. The income is based not only on what you do, but also on the conversion rate that your affiliate receives. So the quality of the product you are selling has a major effect on the commission. As does the sale price of course.

As far as income goes, it varies wildly. There are two major groups of commission rates. The big companies pay roughly 10% or less and the small ones run anywhere from 25% to 50%. The small companies do that to attract the major affiliate marketers. The big companies don't care.

If pushed, I would have to say that income from commission sales should be slightly higher than your advertising income would be. If you aren't really pushing for sales you'll probably run somewhere in the $10 to $200 range depending on your traffic. On the other hand, you certainly can push the results into the $500 or more a month range. In fact, many of the "gurus" rely on making $10,000 plus with a launch. Of course, a commission from a launch isn't an ongoing income. But there are usually enough launches that it may as well be.

For planning purposes though, I'd suggest you reign in your greed and assume you'll make a little bit more than you would if you just advertised. So something in the $10 to $200 range would be more appropriate for planning purposes.

For our purposes, we're going to continue with a consistent 1000 viewers. We're also going to assume a $147 product being paid 50%. This was the typical entry price for affiliate products prior to the recession, although the price dropped drastically in 2010 as the extent of the recession became apparent. If you select your products well, so that they are closely tied to your customer base, you should at least produce Google's response of 0.0054 clicks per view. This means you will get roughly six readers visiting your affiliate's page per month. If your affiliate is able to close 1% of their sales leads then you should average $4.41 per month.

Of course, there is nothing preventing you from maintaining multiple affiliates (thus multiplying the return). Neither is there anything (except your agreement with the affiliate) to prevent you using other means to sell. For example, if you include the product in your routine email marketing you will probably find that you get a much higher response.

Where Can I Get Affiliates

There are three basic methods to find affiliates.

You can:

1. Sign up with your suppliers, teachers, and others you deal with
2. Use affiliate marketing forums, such as the Warrior Forum
3. Actively search for affiliates
4. Use an affiliate matching service such as Clickbank

One of the issues that you need to be very aware of with commission sales is that of trust. Without trust, you will not be able to sell anything. There is a cost for every attempt at selling. You pay that cost out of trust. If you sell anything without that trust being repaid from the sale (and in fact, enhanced), you will eventually lose all your customers. You build trust by solving the customer's problems. You build trust by having people recommend your products. You build trust by giving the customer something they can use. And you spend trust every time you ask the customer to trust you. This applies both to your products (or services) and to those products (and services) you recommend. Stephen Covey referred to this concept as the "Emotional Bank Account".

The best source of affiliates is the people that you have already dealt with. These can be suppliers, teachers, or even people you talk to in blogs and forums. If you were pleased with the products and services you bought from these people, then your customers will also be pleased. Or at least, it's more likely that your customers will be. If they are pleased then you will increase your trust factor enough to overcome the loss in trust from the sales attempt. If the people you deal with sell any product or service, they are a possible affiliate. Typically, you can find an affiliate link on their site or you can simply contact them to ask if they have considered selling through affiliates.

The next best method is to use internet marketing forums such as Warrior Forum. Warrior Forum can be found at http://www.warriorforum.com/. Other marketers (and you will be joining their ranks) use these forums to ask questions and discuss affiliates programs. And affiliates. These forums are a good source of information on the reputation of affiliates and potential affiliates.

Of course, not everything occurs online. If you have the money to attend internet marketing conventions, you can use these occasions as opportunities to network with other marketers. Affiliate marketing (i.e. commission sales) is bound to come up at some point. In fact, rather than say "can use", I would suggest that either "should use" or "must use" would have been more accurate word choices for me to use here.

You can also actively search for affiliates. Visit other blogs on your topic (you should do this anyway), and then use that process to find people who are also selling to your customers. Or as a less desirable alternative, use a search site such as Google or Bing to search for "affiliates".

Finally, you can use affiliate matching services. The most well known of these is Clickbank. In this case, you'll download the whole sales-page, and install it in your site. Then people come to you to buy, pay through Clickbank and Clickbank pays both you and the manufacturers. Other affiliate matching services have more traditional ad rotation processes. However, they all exist to match would-be product publishers with would-be product sellers. Unfortunately, the quality of product on these sites tends to be variable (emphasizing the low end), as does the price paid.

What Are the Advantages of Commission Sales

In many ways, commission sales are just a variation on advertising. And just as this model shares many characteristics with advertising, so it also shares many of the advantages. For example:

1. It is a set and leave system
2. You can use it anywhere.

However, it also has a number of unique advantages when compared to advertising.

For example, you have more control over which affiliates you will be dealing with. With advertising, you are typically dealing with an ad rotator or intermediary of some sort. This person or company determines whose ads they will run. With commission sales, you can determine not only whom you will be dealing with but also which of their products you will be selling. This gives you a chance to focus on more lucrative items and items that complement your offerings.

You also have more alternatives for marketing and selling commission products. You can use a direct link to your affiliate in your email campaigns, for example. With advertising, you are typically not allowed to advertise in emails.

As a result of these two items, commission sales have a much higher upper end than does advertising. Once you've reached your traffic limits, you can continue to improve your commission sales by exercising greater care in selecting affiliates. The result is a much higher high-end to your earnings. With advertising, you have little ability to manipulate maximum earnings. As a result, you are less likely to reach high earnings.

What Are the Disadvantages of Commission Sales

While affiliate marketing for commissions can be very lucrative, it also has many of the downsides of advertising. For example:

1. Low income probability
2. Readers leave your site so you may lose them permanently
3. Payment rules may result in non-payment of earned commissions

For the sake of brevity, I'm not going to repeat the details on these (you can see them described in detail earlier in the book under "advertising").

There are however, a number of disadvantages unique to this method of monetization. At least compared to advertising.

Unless something is sold, you won't receive any income. Where advertising is based on your readers' willingness to click (or their willingness to look at your site), commission sales is based on their willingness to buy. And that's a different thing entirely.

Related to this is the lack of control you have over the process. One result of this lack of control is that in many cases, you have little to no control on what the rules of commission payment are. The seller typically decides the conditions of the affiliation, and what actions of the customer will generate a commission for you.

On the same tack, you have no control over the conversion rates your affiliate has. If they are good with copywriting, they will have an above average conversion.

Some of my sites for example have experienced up to 25% conversion rates. (I only wish I knew why). Others will obviously be much less than the 1% we used in our calculation. While affiliates should tell you in advance what their average conversion rate is, there is no guarantee their figures are accurate. Or that it will apply to your readership.

Finally, the third expression of this lack of control is in the quality of the products being sold. You have little to no control over the quality of product. While you can take care to ensure that products you see meet your standards, most affiliates sell products you don't see. And frankly, the quality of products sold over the internet varies over a wide range from very, very professional to way below substandard. This is especially true with virtual products.

Another problem with this method is that these aren't your customers and it isn't your product. So if you're going to use this technique you need to figure out how to capture opt-in names and emails. Otherwise, you won't be able to establish an ongoing relationship with the customer.

Hints, Tips and Gotchas of Commission Sales

Most of the hints, tips and gotchas of advertising also apply to commission sales. For example:

1. Advertising above the fold
2. Advertising at decision points
3. Avoiding damage to your blog's reputation

After all, you are basically just placing a specific advertisement on your site.

One tip that is specific to commission sales, is to pick your affiliates carefully. You need to identify and pick affiliates whose products are not in direct competition with your own. Yet you also need those products to be of interest to your readership. For example, there is no point in trying to do commission sales with someone selling bug spray if your blog is about living in the city. On the other hand, if you blog about recreational vehicle camping, then an affiliate selling bug spray may be exactly right for your readership.

Chapter 8:

Earning Directly: Selling Products

What Is the Product Sales Model

While you can make a nice income from advertising and commissions, in order to really make an income you need to become active. You need to create your own products and sell them on your blog. Typically, this is done by means of an opt-in page in which you give away an ethical bribe (in other words a "free" product you exchange for an email address and permission to contact) and a set of sales pages or sales letters for each product you have.

One comment -- if you are going to be involved in selling products you need to develop a relationship with your readers. And blogs are great for attracting new readers and getting them interested in you and your products. They're even great for keeping people interested in you. But they rely on someone returning to your store. And that doesn't happen with the internet. To overcome that on the web you need to use a push technique ... i.e. email marketing. In other words, you need to go to them.

I'm not talking about spamming. Spamming, by the way, is no longer legal in Canada, the US or most of the world. Spamming can bring severe penalties if you are charged. Instead, I'm talking about a newsletter in email form, which your potential customers ask to receive. The "ask" being the key. The customer must know that they will be receiving this sales information.

And your customers must be eager to receive your email if you are using email marketing to build your relationship with your customers. The easiest way to do this is to adjust your email campaign. Include more content than sales offers in your campaign. While you need your potential customers to realize that you are in the business of selling to them, giving them free, useful information will give them a reason to trust you.

The basic product sales model is therefore, that I obtain a product, I send traffic to my blog, I use my blog to convince people to exchange their email address for something, then I establish a relationship using the blog and email marketing. Finally, I sell them a product.

What Products Can I Sell

There are three types of products you can provide. These include:

1. Physical products
2. Virtual products
3. Knowledge based products

The first we'll look at are physical products. We've all seen the ecommerce stores that sell cameras or books over the internet. Amazon is probably the most obvious example. eBay is another example. Of course, with your blog you don't need to go overboard. You don't need to have an ecommerce store. An ad on the blog and an order page can be good enough.

On the other side, is the virtual product. These products exist in cyberspace only. They have no existence outside the computer. eBooks are probably the most common example of this, with Amazon's Kindle store being a major retailer. However, other products include software, music, stock trading, in fact, anything that can exist in the ether. Anything that doesn't have to be shipped to the customer.

So far, we've been talking about any type of product. And we've basically covered all products with the classifications we've used. But there is a special type of product which is especially well suited for the internet. I'm talking, of course, about learning content. Also known as knowledge products or information products. These are basically courses in the form of books or eBooks or audios or videos or live events. Or even blogs. You, as an expert, are going to teach someone how to do something. You can do that in the form of a physical or virtual product. Live events are usually physical although the virtual event is becoming more popular. eBooks are virtual products, as are MP3 recordings. Knowledge products are so important they need to be covered separately.

In theory, you can sell any product with your blog. However, in general you want the product to be related to the outer reason for the blog (and thus in the eyes of your reader related to your blog's topic). Otherwise, you will damage your blog's reputation. Effectively, you will be classed as a spammer or ad-rag. Besides, if your reader isn't interested they won't buy. So being consistent increases sales.

How Much Can You Realistically Make from Product Sales

I started off this chapter with the hoary old saw, "If you want to make real money on the web, you need your own products." And it's definitely true -- up to a certain extent. The problem of course, is that you also need to pay for both traffic and development. And if you aren't careful, your cost of traffic and development can easily surpass your sales figures.

Despite this concern, selling products can provide very high income. One person I know is making roughly $240,000 in yearly sales after only five years. So this is a very high income strategy.

Frankly, from this point onwards, determining how much you can make is silly. Bluntly, you have too much control to make any estimates valid. In addition, your customer's responsiveness will have a major effect on the total sales. And of course, no one says you have to have only one product. In fact, you really do need to have a series of products in order to be profitable.

However, for the sake of comparison, let's throw together some figures. Again, we'll be talking about 1000 views per month using two views per customer. This time we're going to presume that you have a complete suite of products: an entry product at $27, an intermediate product at $97, a mid-level product at $297 and a high level product at $1997. With that level of traffic and a reasonably responsive clientele, you should be able to sell one $27 product per week, one $97 and one $297 product per month . Your high level ($1997) product will most likely sell once per quarter. Therefore, you should average around the $568 per month range.

As you can see this is much higher than the income from either an advertisement or from commission sales. Just remember that the numbers are for discussion purposes only. Your own income will vary greatly from these figures.

Unfortunately, this income isn't going to be all yours. You need to deduct the costs of producing the income from the proceeds. And that means you will need to account for the cost of designing, developing and producing the product. If you are using physical products (including CDs), you also need to include the costs of acquisition, storage and shipment.

Where Can I Get Products

You don't have to sell your own products.

There are companies that will design, manufacture, and even ship your products for you. Or any combination of those. There are wholesalers who will ship directly to your customers for you. They'll even provide the order page. The typical description used for these manufacturers is drop-shipper.

Of course, you can also design, develop and manufacture your own products. I'm not going to get into that in this book. But many people choose to do that and are quite successful.

The third option is to arrange with someone else to do one of the steps in the production of a product. For example, you could outsource the production of a product you designed. For example, using voice actors to record courses is becoming common and cost effective. Or you could outsource design. Or you could outsource development or shipping. Or all of the steps, or any combination.

What Are the Advantages of Product Sales

The biggest advantage of product sales is obvious. It is the amount of money that you can make from selling your own products.

In addition, unlike Commission sales, you are selling your own product to your own customer. So, instead of getting a pittance for driving a customer to the sales page, you get 100%.

You also get their name and email so you'll be able to continue to sell them other products. You can use this information to build a greater rapport with your customers. Hopefully, you'll be able to sell them more products. But you can also use this relationship to research which products you should be creating (or obtaining) for them.

And you also open up the possibility of doing your own commission sales. Also called affiliate sales. But this time you're the publisher and the other person is the retailer. When you reach this stage, you will find that your income goes up exponentially. That's why affiliates are willing to give up 50% of their product sales. If you add 2 affiliates, each selling the same amount as you, even at 50% commission you will double your income for the same amount of work.

What Are the Disadvantages of Product Sales

There is one very large problem with this technique. The cost of products. Even if you create your own virtual products, there is a high cost in creating them either in terms of time or in terms of money. In fact, it is easy to get lost in the creation process and not finish. It's also much easier to create a product you aren't happy with than it is to create a product you are proud of. And the rule of "good enough" doesn't help when what you've created really isn't good enough to meet the expectations of your customers.

The second big problem with this technique (beyond the amount of time involved) is that traffic and income are very closely linked. You must have enough traffic to support your product development efforts. And frankly, it takes a lot of traffic to generate a reasonable level of sales.

But if you can pull it off, this is when your blog becomes a real business.

Hints, Tips and Gotchas of Product Sales

Now let's stop here for a second and look at knowledge or content products.

If you listen to the gurus on marketing talk, it's easy as pie to create content. It's easy for them because they don't do it. They hire someone else. All they do is get up and say what they're told to say. Content development associations have developed a rule of thumb that every hour of presentation requires forty hours of preparation. So a one hour educational seminar should take you a week to design, write and practice.

They'll also tell you that nothing is as important as marketing. They're wrong. There are three parts to any business. They are all critical. Marketing, production and administration. Screw up any of them badly enough and your business will fail. You can outsource any of them. Companies do it all the time. As an entrepreneur, your duty is to ensure that all three are done. And done correctly. Blow it and your business will suffer and probably fail. Get all three right, and your business will succeed. It's as simple as that.

My focus is on teaching you how to create blog versions of knowledge products. That's what blogging is. And to be more precise, in this book I'm focusing on monetizing your blog. If you want to learn how to create learning content in general -- properly -- then I suggest you visit http://www.learningcreators.com . That blog and its products focus on creating courses, books and eBooks and other learning content products.

Chapter 9:

Earning Directly: Selling Services

What Is the Service Sales Model

Products are one offering that you can sell. But just as you can sell products with your blog, you can sell services too. The process and the model are essentially the same. The only real difference being that the product is a service.

With this model, you blog to increase awareness and to build credibility. You then use the blog to drive a potential client to the opt-in page. You then use the potential client's email to build a relationship and ultimately convince them to buy your service.

In many cases, however, this process is shortened by the use of a taste of the service. For example, if you are offering coaching you might offer a 20-minute free coaching call. This allows you to do personal selling to convince the potential customer to buy your service.

What Services Can I Sell

In theory, almost any service can be sold using a blog. After all, the only real difference between selling services directly and selling them indirectly is that your blog is expected to take the order. However, delivering the service can be an issue. Many services require physical access to the product being serviced. This is fine if the product is located locally. However, unless the product being serviced can be shipped, it is a problem if the product is not local.

Other services, on the other hand, do not involve a physical element. For example, accounting services, bookkeeping services, legal services, search engine marketing, software development, personal help, and consulting all involve communications and knowledge rather than a local presence. So they are perfect candidates for selling over the web using a blog.

How Can I Deliver Services

Local services are a great thing to sell with a blog. In essence, what you are doing is using your blog to drive customers to your bricks and mortar store. Your blog can sell your customers on furnace repair or car repairs or windshield repair or tax calculation or whatever other service you provide. It can even take the orders for the service. Selling local services actually has an advantage since local search tends to be easier to dominate than the old-style national or global search.

However, you can also provide the service remotely. Website maintenance, social marketing, and search engine marketing are traditionally provided this way. The advantage is that you can sell around the world, which means even a small part of the available market can be quite large.

Coaching is one major way to provide services remotely. In essence, you use a teleconferencing service -- and yes, there are some free ones -- some very good free ones -- and run group coaching calls. Or use the phone and do individual phone coaching. Or use email if that's what you

97

want to do. And of course, you can sell coaching on almost any topic.

One of the best services to sell is the group coaching program. With this type of program, you arrange a teleconference call between yourself and all the individuals that purchase the program. The call typically consists of a mix of questions and answers, problem resolution, and guided learning.

How Much Can You Realistically Make from Service Sales

The problem with any service is the ability to scale the service. In other words, the ability to sell multiple copies without adding more of your time. After all, you only have a limited amount of time available.

The prices, and the willingness of your customers to purchase a service from you depends entirely on your niche and your ability to convince your customers to trust you. How much you charge depends almost entirely on how much they value that service.

However, for our purposes, we're going to presume that you will be using the group coaching method with a weekly teleconference call. We're also going to presume that customers sign up for ten months and then begin to filter away. This is typical for recurring payment programs. A group coaching program such as this typically will sell for $97 per month although there can be a large variation (even up to $497 or higher). Based on our 1000 visitors a month model, you should be able to sell at least one new coaching program per month. That means by the eleventh month, you should be earning about $970 per month (in other words you will have 10 customers).

What Are the Advantages of Service Sales

The biggest advantage is the amount of income that can be earned. It is often more difficult to sell a service. And scaling that service can be even harder. However, if a method of scaling the service is found, there is a greater potential for high value income than even product sales.

In addition, service sales also share the same advantages as selling your own products. These are:

1. You are selling your own product to your own customer
2. You receive 100% of the income
3. You have your customer's name and email so you'll be able to continue to sell them other products and services.
4. You can also use this relationship to research which products you should be creating (or obtaining) for them
5. You are able to package the services and do your own commission sales

What Are the Disadvantages of Service Sales

Just as service sales and product sales share the same advantages, they also share the same disadvantages. More specifically:

1. Cost
2. Importance of traffic on sales

However, there are also a number of disadvantages specific to service sales.

While some services (such as group coaching) can be scaled, many services cannot. You have a very definite limit to the number of customers that can be serviced. A problem that product sales does not have.

Services are often more difficult to visualize. This makes selling them more difficult. Which in turn means you need to have your sales copy functioning at its best.

Hints, Tips and Gotchas of Service Sales

Selling services through your blog can be the most lucrative way to use your blog -- if done right. To get the most from this you do need to follow a few rules.

Always be looking for ways to scale your business. One of the problems with any service is that it can be difficult to scale. As you add new customers, there is a point at which you are no longer able to service those customers. Long before that point, you will find that your quality of service degrades. This is to be avoided at all costs. With services, you need to be innovative in looking for new ways to provide the service that don't require more service resources (i.e. time).

On the other hand, services don't work well when sold remotely. You need to consider how best to deliver your services from a distance. Selling over the internet is a global proposition. Although you can sell locally, this isn't really making best use of the characteristics of the web. You need to restructure your service delivery to allow you to sell to people who are around the world. For example, if you are selling coaching services, rather than delivering face-to-face coaching, try to restructure your program into a guided learning program delivered by phone. Or perhaps as a webinar.

One of the big problems with services is their cost to value to price ratios. It is important that you keep your service costs under control. Your price will be the source of pushback from your clients. While you can use value to adjust that perception of the appropriate price, you will still find that your price is not elastic. An inelastic price simply means a price that you can't increase easily. As a result, you will need to keep your costs of providing the service under control. Look for ways to share the cost. This can also help you scale the offering.

Finally, because services can't be visualized you need to be very clear in your sales materials. To do that you need to start from a very clear understanding of what benefits your services provide. And you need to be able to articulate those benefits clearly in words that your readership will understand and believe.

Chapter 10:

Earning Directly: Selling Access

What Is the Access Sales Model

Now so far, we've talked about using your blog to sell something else. You may be making money directly from the sale or you may be making it indirectly by advertising for the sale. But you're selling something else other than the blog.

Selling access is one way that you can sell the blog itself.

There are many variations on selling access. You may be selling access to a service such as coaching (although I actually covered that as selling a service). Or you may sell access to knowledge -- such as a blog. Or access to a software tool. The common theme however, is that ownership of the product or service does not change hands. The customer is buying the use of the product for a period of time.

You may have several levels of access. Including some that are free. Blog memberships often work that way. The basic blog article is free, but every week or so there is a premium article that treats the subject in depth. To access this premium content you need to pay for a membership.

What Can I Sell Access To

You can sell access to almost anything. Physical products aren't usually sold that way -- although a car rental for example could be considered as an access sale. However, virtual products and knowledge are perfect for this model. Blogs, courses, articles, eBooks, and online software tools are often sold using this method.

One common use of an access sale is the opt-in membership. With this concept, a paragraph or two of an article is available to the public. However, you can't access the rest of the article without registering -- which of course, means opting-in to the publisher's email campaign.

How Much Can You Realistically Make from Selling Access

Because memberships are generally recurring, they are typically priced using the recurring billing model. As a result, they are great as income producers. Even a one or two dollar access product can result in large monthly sales. One hundred people buying a ten dollar membership is the equivalent of one person buying a one thousand dollar product per month. And it is considerably easier to sell.

In our service sales discussion, we actually used an access sale. So we can use those figures. In fact, the amount is dependent on the type of products we sell. A typical blog membership, would sell for much less than the $97 per month of the coaching example. $29 and $47 are more common price points for access to course, product or blog. However, in at least one case, I have seen prices of $227 per month. Using the $47 price point, it is likely that two sales per month could be made with the 1000 visitors. If that is the case, the monthly sales should be in the area of $940 per month after the tenth month.

Where Can I Get Content

This is a course on making money from your blog, not a course on how to blog so I'm going to deal with this on a very superficial level.

Each type of product you are giving access to has a different source. You can either create the content yourself (the best method), you can outsource the content creation (meaning you control the quality), or you can buy the content. In the chapter on selling products, I discussed how to get training content you develop yourself.

When blogging I recommend using the content marketing method. With that method, you produce a mix of different types of content. Some content will be high quality. Some will be of traffic quality.

If you are seeking to make money from selling access to your blog then you will need to produce two different types of high quality content. One will be given away as free information. This will help to convince your readers that the hidden content is worth paying for. The second version of high quality content is your premium content. This is what the readers will pay to access. In this case, traffic quality content will be used only for the purposes of article, video or podcast marketing. You will want to keep it away from the blog because it will reduce the value of the blog. In its place, you can consider republishing content from article repositories, guest posters or personal opinion pieces.

What Are the Advantages of Selling Access

There are five major advantages to selling access.

The first is that access programs typically use a recurring payment model. This pricing model will provide the highest returns of all the techniques.

Secondly, it is relatively easy and less costly in terms of time, energy and sometimes money. Typically, much of the content is being produced regardless. You are simply converting it from a one-time payment model to a recurring pricing model.

The third advantage is that less effort is needed to sell access programs because the price is much lower than a one-time or loan payment pricing model would be.

One of the biggest advantages is that you don't need to produce the content until you need to deliver it. Of course, you should be several weeks ahead of schedule, but in theory, if necessary you can prepare it just prior to the first customer needing it. This is much more convenient than having to design, produce and publish the whole product before you can begin selling it.

Finally, this type of product leaves the ownership of the product in your hands. In theory, unless your customer is current in paying for access, they will not be able to access the information.

What Are the Disadvantages of Selling Access

The only real problem with selling access is that with an access-based membership -- such as access to blog entries -- you need to be constantly producing high value content. You won't be able to use the typical blog or traffic quality content. You need real article level content. And that can be expensive in terms of both time and money.

If you intend to sell access to your blog, the second thing you cannot afford is to produce content on an erratic schedule. You need to have a firm, definite schedule on which content is published.

Hints, Tips and Gotchas of Selling Access

To ensure a firm, definite publication schedule you need to establish an editorial schedule. When starting the access portion of your blog, lay out ten months of content. You don't need to be complete. And you don't need to stick to your list. But you do need to ensure that you have a list of topics that will provide ten months' worth of content. That means if you are publishing one paid content piece per week you will need roughly 40 topics or titles.

Next, determine how far in advance you need to stay. Typically, one month is sufficient but it will vary from situation to situation. You will need to have only one week's content ready before you launch the access as a product. However, you will need to have enough content ready prior to the first sale to ensure that you are always ahead of your advance. For example, suppose our access program was based on one paid article per week. Further, we decide that we need to be one month ahead of our dates. In that case, we could begin the sales launch as soon as we had one article (i.e. one week's worth of content). However, we would need to complete another three weeks' worth of articles before the first customer is activated. After that, we would only need to average one article per week. If we produce two in one week, we can safely skip a week.

Keeping an advanced editorial schedule is necessary in order to ensure that publication always occurs on the same day. Unfortunately, things happen. Writing can't be finished on time. Writing doesn't get started when it should. The editorial advance allows us to keep to a consistent publication schedule even when we are unable to produce to a consistent schedule.

Effectively it gives us a buffer to absorb any delivery problems.

Chapter 11:

Earning Indirectly

What Do We Mean by Earning Indirectly from Your Blog?

While making money from our blogs is all well and good, there are other ways to make your blog pay for itself.

For example, we can use the indirect strategy. In this strategy, you are not using the blog to make money. Rather you are using it as a marketing tool. Whatever you are selling with the blog is what you will make money on. Think of it as the "blog as a cost of sales" or "blog as advertising" strategy.

There are two major variations or examples of this technique. The first is expert marketing and the second is in support of bricks and mortar sales.

Expert marketing is a technique for selling based on improving your standing in the opinion of your potential clients. We have a free introductory course on it on TrainingNOW.ca. You can find it at http://ww2.trainingnow.ca/expert-marketing-128. The tagline we use for it is "Becoming the one to call" and that's the essence of the technique. Essentially, you are going to market your product or service by convincing your potential customers that you are *THE* expert in that field. Once you've built up your reputation in that arena, any recommendations you make -- i.e. products or services you sell -- will automatically become the benchmark.

Have you heard of the Wealthy Barber? David Chilton was a mutual funds salesman who used this technique to boost his investment business. Now he's no longer selling mutual funds for himself. Another example is Phil Edmundson. He was a reporter until he wrote Lemonaid. As a result of this book, he became a consumer advocate, an associate of Ralph Nader, and an expert witness in automobile court cases. Now he lives on a beach in Panama.

With bricks and mortar sales, you are actually selling a product from your physical store. This is very much the traditional view of having a web presence. In essence, the actual selling/production/distribution process is occurring off-line. The blog is used primarily as a driver of traffic and as a platform for traditional sales practices.

Generally speaking, you'll use an indirect method because it is a pre-made decision. You choose it because you have little choice or because it is critical to the decision to blog at all. You've already got the business in place. Or you're out of work. Or you're looking for employees. And so on.

In this case, blogging is just a different form of advertising and as such, you're going to consider it a cost of doing business. All the money is coming from your main business and the blog is just there to drive traffic to the main business. Or, of course, to support converting leads into sales.

Your measure of the blog then, is how effective the blog is in generating new customers, converting leads to sales or whatever your purpose is in having a blog.

The around blogging strategy has the potential to produce the most income. However, the indirect strategy is far more likely to produce slightly less income although still more than other options. After all, you're presumably already making a high income from your business or profession. And this strategy is simply adding more income.

So in this case, we tend to decide to blog in order to make more money. Unlike the other cases where we decide how to make money with the blog after we've already decided to blog.

Let's take a little closer look at the first of these variations we identified -- expert marketing.

Chapter 12:

Earning Indirectly: Expert Marketing

What Is Expert Marketing

Expert marketing has a number of related concepts and alternative names. For example, personal branding is one version of expert marketing. Reputation marketing and repair are related concepts and techniques.

Simply put, expert marketing focuses on creating a brand for yourself, which makes you the person to call. It is a series of techniques focused on getting recognition for your expertise in your field. Some people think it is all about calling yourself an expert. However, if you do so you will have lost. What you are trying to do with expert marketing, is to get other people to refer to you as the expert in your field. For example, if you think of self-help gurus you automatically think of Tony Robbins.

Most expert marketing techniques work by giving the potential customer a taste of your abilities. Similar to the sample tables at your local grocery or Costco. This taste can be in the form of articles, books, blogs, videos or other content.

If you are using expert marketing there is usually one of three groups of actions behind the marketing.

You could be hunting for a job. You're out of work and you need to convince an employer that they should be calling you. That you know how to solve their issues. To a certain extent, your blog acts as a supplement to the traditional resume. A sample sheet if you will, aimed at the manager rather than at the human resources department.

Or it could be the other way around. You could be the employer hunting for the right type of employee. Rather than attract everyone and his brother, you might use the blog to demonstrate your expertise as an organization. This means you are more likely to attract senior individuals since the others are likely to realize they won't be selected.

The third alternative is essentially the same as a job hunt. However, in this case, you are using the blog to look for customers rather than looking for an employer. Consultants and contractors often use this alternative. Since their bread and butter is their knowledge, expert marketing through a blog and a set of white papers is an excellent method of convincing potential customers of the consultant's capability.

What Can I Sell With Expert Marketing

In many ways, blogging is expert marketing by definition. The whole idea behind expert marketing is to convince the audience that you can solve their problem by providing samples of your knowledge. Whatever their problem happens to be (at least within the topic area), you can find a solution to it. As a result, you can sell virtually anything using this technique. Although you may need to rethink what you are selling or how you sell it. In fact, with expert marketing what you are selling is yourself -- the product or service is incidental.

For example, you might sell cars. For the sake of silliness, let's pick Ford cars. (I wish I could say keeping it in the family but no such luck!) You might create a blog discussing different makes and models of cars. You might discuss how to choose a make and model of car. You might talk about budgeting for a vehicle and preparing for the inevitable breakdowns. You might compare the strengths and weaknesses of different makes and models. You might discuss the history of the motor car.

The point of this exercise is to convince people that you know everything there is about choosing a car. When you then go ahead and recommend a Ford Fairlane for them, your customers will automatically believe you are picking the best vehicle for their particular situation. (Not that anyone would. I don't think they make that particular model anymore, do they?)

Of course, it is much easier to sell services with this technique since most services are based on knowledge. Expert marketing is based on proving you have the knowledge to solve their problems. Either to choose the solution or implement the solution. So any product based in knowledge (e.g. services) is very closely connected to this technique.

How Much Can You Realistically Make with Expert Marketing

So far, I've been able to create a reasonable example based on our 1000 visitors per month traffic estimate. However, this is where my ability to estimate completely breaks down. For example, if you are capturing 25% of the visitors and converting 1% of those, you may increase your sales by three sales per month. If you are selling a car for example, that might represent $100,000 in sales. On the other hand, if you are selling books, that might represent only $30 per month.

Expert marketing (and all the indirect marketing methods) are advertising expenses. While they can be traced to specific sales -- and you should keep track of their conversion rates -- estimating their value depends entirely on you and your product or service. And your ability to convince your customer of your abilities.

Where Can I Get Expert Marketing Content

Blogging is by definition a form of expert marketing. The big difference is that in this case, we are being explicit here in stating that we are not directly selling with the blog. Therefore, you can get expert content wherever you get your regular blog content.

Typically, however, you will want to ensure that you use only high quality content on your blog. In fact, the higher quality the content, the better. The principal choices you have are:

1. Write it yourself
2. Outsource the writing (based on your outline)
3. Guest bloggers
4. Content repositories (such as EzineArticles.com)

While traffic quality content can be used for generating traffic, it should be used with extreme care. Traffic quality content which approaches high quality can be safely used. However, typical traffic quality content and especially the lower ranges of traffic quality may work to reduce the effectiveness of your expert marketing efforts. It may even convince your customers that you aren't a real expert.

I'm not a big fan of using subpar traffic quality content for anything. However, subpar traffic quality should always be avoided for this technique.

What Are the Advantages of Expert Marketing

There are a number of advantages to using a blog and expert marketing. Expert marketing uses content marketing to achieve a particular goal -- namely building your reputation. Basically, we're talking targeting your brand marketing.

Expert marketing is one of the most powerful types of marketing. By convincing others that you have a particular skill, you help to convince them that you can solve their problems. The emphasis here is on the plural.

This perception of world-class expertise will allow you to charge a premium rate for anything you do. If you sell consulting services, you can increase both the quantity and price of your services. You'll also be able to add more lucrative services, such as keynote speaking. If you sell products, you'll be able to sell more expensive products and often you'll be able to charge a premium for the products you sell.

What Are the Disadvantages of Expert Marketing

Expert marketing may appear to be the perfect marketing method. However, it does have four primary disadvantages:

1. Need for high quality content
2. Need to be consistent in quality and frequency
3. Need for modesty
4. May price you out of the market

Maintaining a reputation as an expert requires a constant supply of high-quality content. While traffic quality content can be used for traffic purposes, it must be done with care. Used improperly it will damage your reputation. Subpar traffic quality content should never be used as it can damage the reputation you are trying to build. While I never suggest the use of subpar quality content, it is absolutely imperative that you avoid any connection with bad quality content. Your reputation will be affected well beyond any improvement in your traffic could possibly justify.

Continuing on that theme, you will need to be consistent with your blogging. As I've already indicated, this definitely applies to the high-quality content you provide. However, it also applies to the frequency with which you publish your blog articles. Although you have a slight advantage in flexibility over some alternatives, your readers must be able to rely on your blog to have a new, high quality entry whenever they check back. Or they will forget to check back.

Whenever you are marketing, there is a tendency to brag. It's hard not to. After all, you are trying to convince the reader that you have a particular characteristic. Saying it outright is always a temptation. With expert marketing, that is the kiss of death. The moment you state that you are an expert in a particular area your readers will begin to question your ability. You need to focus on proving your expertise without ever saying that is what you are doing. This discipline can be harder to maintain than it might seem at first glance.

The fact that expert marketing can increase your ability to charge extra is a two-edged sword. Although you may be able to charge more, you may find that fewer customers will call you. The reason that you can charge more is that your customers will start with the belief that you charge a premium. Unfortunately, some people are unwilling (or unable) to pay a premium. So they won't call you no matter how much you try to convince them that you do not charge a premium. People have been known to decide your competition charges too much, rather than admit your price is the same as someone with less skill in their opinion.

Hints, Tips and Gotchas of Expert Marketing

Many of the tips for this strategy have already been covered in detail in previous chapters. However, there are four key hints that you need to consider.

1. Need to establish an editing schedule
2. Need to focus on high quality content
3. Beware of traffic quality content
4. Avoid subpar traffic quality content

In order to ensure that you have consistency in your quality and frequency of publishing you will need to create an editing schedule. You will need to write several weeks' worth of high quality articles prior to launching your blog. This will allow you to maintain an average delivery schedule without having to worry about falling behind on those inevitable weeks when you are less productive.

I know that I've mentioned quality content before. But it is imperative you realize how important this is. (Sorry if you're getting a headache from me beating you over the head with this).

Because you are using the articles to build your reputation, you need to be very concerned about the quality of anything you publish. Your reputation is directly affected by the quality of the content you are associated with. Whatever the reason behind the content!

You need to be producing consistently high quality content. This means that you will need to pay more for the content. If you're spending time rather than money, it means that you will need to spend more time and care on the content. If you are buying the content, you will need to deal with writers who are able to deliver higher quality articles. And pay their prices.

One of the techniques that is used to control costs is to use lower quality content for traffic purposes with article, video or podcast marketing. Unfortunately, this is dangerous when performing expert marketing. There is always the possibility that you will damage your reputation. So great care must be used when working with traffic quality content.

We've all seen subpar traffic quality content. That's the type of content that has very obviously been written by someone whose first language is not English (or whatever language you are using). It frequently has spelling errors, grammatical errors and typically looks like someone produced 400 words without having a topic. What they did have was a thesaurus but no dictionary. Frequently these are actually produced by computer using a technique called spinning. They make my 13 year old daughter's homework look good!

I never suggest using subpar traffic quality content -- for anything. Even if you aren't using expert marketing, your blog's reputation is closely tied to the quality of everything you publish. But if you are using expert marketing there is one definite rule that you never want to break. Don't use subpar traffic quality content. Ever. For anything. It will ruin your reputation. And any attempt at expert marketing will fail.

Chapter 13:

Earning Indirectly: Sales Support

What Is Sales Support

A blog can help you sell at most of the points in your sales funnel. If you haven't heard that term before, a sales funnel is simply the set of steps your customers go through as they move from being interested to having purchased your product. This is true regardless of whether you are a "bricks and mortar", a "bricks and clicks" or an ecommerce operation. However, we've already covered the latter two earlier in the book under the topic of "earning directly". So this chapter is going to focus on supporting "bricks and mortar" sales efforts.

For example, a blog can help you attract targeted clients. A blog can be a core element in your keyword/search engine optimization strategy. If you constantly repeat a keyword sequence in your blog, you will find your ratings for that keyword sequence improve. At least up to a point. Match that with references from other websites and you will find your site closer to that critical top ten or first page. Having your site close to the top of your keyword search phrases means that you'll capture more and better targeted leads.

You can argue that expert marketing works no matter what your product or service. However, not everyone wants to engage in expert marketing. Similarly, not everyone wants to sell product or services over the internet. If this is the case, a blog can still work as a platform for more traditional sales and sales support messages.

I'm not going to repeat what was said under expert marketing. Suffice it to say that regardless of whether you are promoting your ability or the product itself, a blog can help you to get on the first page of the search engines both locally and internationally so that you will generate leads. And hopefully sales from those leads. This also applies to post-sale support efforts.

However, in addition to being a sales message, your blog can also act as the platform for traditional post-sales and order entry activities. Just as a regular or ecommerce site can provide order tracking capabilities to internal and external staff and customers, so can a blog. And that includes payment capabilities as well.

Being on Google's front page means having your potential customer's attention. But that isn't enough. You need to convert that attention to desire and trust. Your blog can help do that as well, by proving your capabilities. Your blog can show people that you are an expert and can be trusted. Trust built this way can help in any of the early stages of sales especially the pre-sales and critical first stages of relationship building.

You'll also find that a blog can help you cut down on your costs for post-sales support. For example, your posts might answer specific questions that your clients have. Your blog might also help to convince your customers that you have the answers they need as they become more experienced with your products.

What Can I Sell With Sales Support

Anything that requires sales support can benefit from using a blog for sales support. It doesn't matter if you are selling products, services or access. If there is any support required -- pre-sales, post-sales or order entry, a blog can aid in providing that support.

What Products Work Best with Sales Support

Although any product can benefit from using a blog for sales support there are some products and services that work better than others. For example, sales support works best:

1. With shippable or virtual products or remote services
2. Where customers have many questions but they're all the same set of questions
3. Where leads ask questions before buying in order to decide which version to buy
4. When you want to give customers control -- e.g. in setting appointments.

As in most sales situations, people like to be able to buy as soon as they decide. Actually, they also like to receive the product or service as soon as they decide. As a result, all web sales work best when selling products which are shippable or virtual or for services which can be delivered remotely. Blogging for sales support is no different.

Blogging allows you to add and change advice. It also allows you to make advice reasonably detailed. However, what it doesn't do is allow you to adjust your advice based on the question being asked. Therefore sales support works best when you have a limited number of questions that are asked. On the other hand, your savings from not using people to support your customers increases with the number of questions asked. Therefore, the best value from a blog performing your sales support is when a large number of people arc asking the same questions.

In any sales situation, there is a certain amount of buyer education. Blogs work well for sales support when the amount of buyer education is quite sizable. However, they are not a substitute for a specialist's advice. They stop working when it is necessary to use a specialist's advice before buying. A blog cannot replace a doctor or pharmacist for example.

133

Using blogs for sales support also works well in any case where you want to give the customer control. For example, many garages now allow the customer to book appointments online. Everyone has a need for control. By giving this control to the customer, you are eliminating customer support and letting the customer believe they have control over the situation.

How Much Can You Realistically Make with Sales Support

The whole question of how much you can make by blogging for sales support is somewhat spurious. Sales support is a cost of doing business. It is really a question of how much you are paying for this element of your business. Using a blog to drive your sales support can improve the effectiveness of your sales support functions. It can also greatly reduce the cost of providing those services. Typically, this cost saving far exceeds the cost of blogging.

What Are the Advantages of Sales Support

Using your blog for sales support gives your customer control. For example, your customer can easily pick their own appointment times and dates. This is especially important when your service creates some form of imposition on the customer. By having control themselves, they are less likely to take out their anger on a customer service representative. The design of your software can aid in defusing this anger or it can make it much worse.

In any case, using the web to perform many of the sales support functions can reduce your costs for selling. By providing advice and assistance, your blog can reduce the amount of time spent by your customer service staff.

Of course, these are really advantages provided by sales support and selling over the web. However, there are a number of advantages to using a blog to provide these services. These advantages are associated with using a blogging platform over traditional static websltes.

First, the age of the information will affect the site's rating with search engines. The older the site, the better the rating. The older the page -- and the information on the page -- the worse the rating. So you want your sites to be refreshed with new and additional pages as frequently as possible. A blog makes refreshing the site easier and adding content much easier than it is with traditional HTML based sites.

Second, a site based on blogging software requires much less maintenance than a traditional HTML based site. It's just plain easier to use. A traditional HTML site requires the use of programming staff to code and publish. Even if you are doing the coding using a WYSIWYG (what you see is what you get) tool, you are coding. Certainly, the more complex the coding the more you require professional help. A blog, on the other hand is designed to be maintained by the non-programmer. The software functions similar to a word processing program. Only if you choose to go beyond what is generally available, will you need advanced knowledge.

What Are the Disadvantages of Sales Support

The biggest disadvantage with using a blog is that you are not sending people directly to your sales page. You'll be sending them to a blog page with a link to your sales page. Your readers will then have to choose to click on the link in order to look at your sales page. Whenever you have an extra click, you are going to lose a percentage of people.

In addition, you will not be using the website to its maximum advantage. Because the focus is on supporting the sale rather than selling, you will be unlikely to pick up new leads from your actions. Having said that, there are many reasons you may decide to restrict your website to supporting the sale rather than performing the sale.

Hints, Tips and Gotchas of Sales Support

Providing sales support is one of the oldest uses of the web. Blogging simply makes it easier. However, just as using traditional websites well involves knowing what one is doing, so does using a blog.

It begins with knowing your sales funnel well. How do people move through the funnel? What stages are they going through? What information do they need at each stage? What questions do they have? Your answers will guide your blog. And if those answers are not correct then you will not get the most out of your blog.

Creating any website, including a blog, involves a great deal of work. This work must be justified and guided. You need to know why you are doing this. You need to know what you are hoping to accomplish. You need a set of specific, measurable objectives.

Of course, with sales support more than any other type of blog, you must have the customer visiting and using it to be successful. Simply put there must be more in it for the customer when they use the blog than if they were to simply call your customer service. Otherwise, your customer will continue to call your customer service group and you won't get any benefit from your blog. So you need to build your blog with your customer always at the front of your mind. You need your blog to be valuable to your customer.

On the other hand, no matter how valuable the site, if it is hard to use, your customer is going to feel there is little value in it. So you need to build your blog in a way that helps your customer to find information and to move easily throughout the blog to find the information they need.

Chapter 14:

Earning Around Blogging

What is Earning Around Blogging?

So far, I've been focused on your blog as the moneymaker or on your blog as advertising. However, that's very short sighted. Another strategy takes a much wider view. I call it the "Around the Blog" strategy. It focuses on selling things associated with blogging rather than on a single blog.

You can monetize "around the blog" in two basic ways.

You can sell a service that supports or works with blogging or supports those who blog. Effectively you can help people to blog by getting them ready for blogging. There are many ways you can do that; from helping with installation of a blog to providing customization to providing content to providing training or writing books.

You can also sell products associated with blogging. Most of the blogging software now is designed to be customized. It uses themes to manage the look of the blog. It uses plugins to implement functions which aren't in the basic package. You can provide those products. To take it to the silly extreme you could even sell "I Blog" t-shirts and coffee mugs.

This strategy is all about making money with services or products that are about blogging in general rather than this particular blog or its topic.

Making money around blogging, at least in the more lucrative versions, is very much skills based. That means either you have the skills or you hire someone with the skills. If you don't have the skills or access to the skills, you're pretty well cut out of this market. So if your skills with the web and web programming aren't up to building themes and plugin then it may mean you shouldn't be in this market. Keep in mind that you can outsource i.e. spend money rather than time. It's probably not suggested as an easy way to make money, if you can't do it yourself. However, it is possible.

One thing to keep in mind with making money around blogging, is that you need to be prepared to drive traffic. Even more than any other technique. The good side, is that you can use WordPress or one of the other blogging tools to help drive traffic. So you've got an extra channel for some of the products and services. The exception is if you are competing with the blogging tool's own services.

This is the most time intensive choice. Any of the techniques within this strategy are. Again, you can trade money for time but you will need to invest the most time. The products have a very short lifespan. So you will be constantly revising them.

On the other hand, this can produce the most income if you're successful. It does however, require building a proper business. Basically, you're running a bricks and mortar business where sales are made over the web. This is often referred to as a bricks and clicks business model.

Chapter 15:

Earning Around Blogging:
Selling Services

What Is Earning Around Blogging by Selling Services

As I've said, earning around blogging is a matter of selling products or services related to blogging, to people who wish to blog. Most of the current blogging tools are open source. So the software is frequently free (or nearly so). Most open source projects make their money by selling services for installing the software, customizing the software, integrating the software and maintaining the software.

You can do this too!

What Can I Sell as a Blogging Services

The number of services that can be sold is only limited by your imagination and skill set.

For example, you might install and set up WordPress or Blogger or one of the other blogging software platforms for paying clients. This installation could be in a basic or complete turnkey format. For example, you could sell hosting, where you supply a site with WordPress pre-installed (in other words a very basic installation). The customer is expected to customize it with a theme, plug-ins and content. On the other hand, you might include a flexible theme and a selection of plug-ins that will be needed (that's what we mean by a turnkey system). Along the way, you might even get into customization of your customers' blogs. You might even do all those little tweaks that no one has bothered to write a theme or plug-in for. The term "turnkey" is pretty flexible and you'll have a large universe to choose from.

You could even design sites for others. This could be a matter of identifying what pages and posts are needed. Or it could involve defining or creating the graphics or content.

144

Webhosting is a service that could be provided on a number of levels. You could be a complete ISP. Or you could sub-let your site out as a hosting service. You could focus on setting up sites specific to blogging. Or let your customers set up whatever they need.

You could sell consulting such as search engine optimization or social marketing services. Or advice on blogging. Or you could create training courses on blogging. This is essentially what we're doing with http://www.howdoyoublog.biz.

The possibilities are endless. I've listed only a few here. I'm sure that as you continue blogging you can find other things that you wish were easily available. Each of those is a potential blogging service you could sell.

What Works Best as Blogging Services

The number and type of services that you can provide is only limited by your own skill set and imagination. However there are two characteristics that describe a service that is well suited for this type of selling.

145

Because this is (presumably) web based sales it works best if you remember that your potential clientele can exist anywhere in the world. The best services are any service that you can deliver remotely (that is from a location other than your client's). This allows you to sell anywhere in the world and to build your customer list based on the whole of the market rather than only that which is local to you.

The second issue has to do with the fact that you will be dealing with open source projects. Most of these projects make their money from services rather than the software. For example, hosting and support are the two most popular methods. When selling blogging services being able to connect with the software project -- and having them promote your services -- is an important marketing technique. You therefore want to avoid direct competition with their services, as they will be less willing to promote your services.

How Much Can You Realistically Make with Blogging Services

Just as with products, this question has no answer. In theory, the market is open-ended. However, in practical terms your market will be limited to those companies that are willing to pay someone to perform the work for them.

What Are the Advantages of Selling Blogging Services

Selling services for anything has both good and bad elements.

Most of the methods of monetizing blogs and blogging are low value. That is they have a low return initially and build slowly as the blog begins to take hold with your readership. They are very dependent on volume.

On the other hand, getting a reasonable income quickly is quite possible when selling blogging services. Many of the services are either premium or high priced from the beginning. All it takes to begin the process of making money is one customer. This customer will typically pay all the costs of providing the service. Including the overheads. Therefore, subsequent customers incur only the cost of additional labor. The remaining amount is gross profit.

Because blogging is core to many companies' internet marketing programs, your services will be central to their marketing. This means you can prove yourself very early in their progression. As a result, you can then sell related services to them from a position of strength. After all, you've already proven that you can handle their blogging needs so a leap to copywriting or brochure production or search engine marketing isn't that hard to imagine.

The other advantage is that your principal customer group will have money to spend. And they don't want to (or can't) do the work themselves. This means that your clients will want to hire you from the beginning. All you need to do is place yourself in their field of view. When they know who you are and what you are providing they will buy.

Finally, making the pot even sweeter is the frequency of change that most of the blogging software providers go through. This constant change in the underlying software means that your clients will need to maintain contact with you. After all, you'll need to make changes to their site frequently. This means that you could have a consistent stream of work from a very small pool of clients.

What Are the Disadvantages of Selling Blogging Services

Of course, selling blogging services isn't all fun and games and the road to El Dorado. There are difficulties and disadvantages to this strategy.

Selling services is very much a knowledge game. Unless you know the subject matter very, very well, you probably shouldn't be in the business. After all, you are going to be responsible for managing and directing the provision of those services at a minimum. You will need to be able to identify opportunities and threats. And you will need to give direction to those people who will be doing the actual work.

Knowledge, of course, isn't enough. You also need the skills necessary to perform the services. The good news is that you don't need to have those skills yourself. Unfortunately, you do need to be able to obtain those skills either by outsourcing, partnering or hiring.

Once you have the appropriate knowledge and skills, you still face a number of difficulties. Services don't scale particularly well. There is an upper limit to the amount of service you can provide without having to build a hierarchy with all the attendant problems. As a result, the amount of money you can earn through blogging services has an upper limit.

Making matters worse is the amount of time and energy that you may waste inappropriately on leads. While many people use blogging software -- and therefore are potential candidates for blogging services -- most will never purchase your services. Blogging software is generally open-source, so it tends to attract those who are unwilling to spend money. These people will be just as unwilling to purchase services from you. You will find that the best customers are businesses. However, the majority of people inquiring will be individuals.

Complicating matters even further is that margins, generally speaking, are cut thin. Since the services are delivered remotely, there is a tendency to purchase those services from countries where the standard of living (and the cost) is much lower than in the developed world. In addition, there is a belief that using the product makes you an expert in the related services. You will often find that you are competing against high school, college and university students and part-time individuals who consider themselves well paid at minimum wage.

Hints, Tips and Gotchas of Selling Blogging Services

More than any other option except expert marketing, this is reputation based selling. In essence, you are going to be selling your ability to deliver. As a result, expert marketing is the best way to sell blogging services. However, all the expert marketing in the world won't help you if you don't deliver. And you can't deliver if you don't have the knowledge and skills needed. So before you start, make sure that you have those skills or don't choose this option.

Of course, you don't have to do everything yourself. You can hire the skills. All you need is the ability to do it yourself if you needed to. Why do you need the skills if you aren't going to be doing the work yourself? Because you can't afford to have your representatives ruin your reputation. This means you need to be very, very careful in who you outsource to. This includes all forms of hiring individuals or companies to do the work. And you can't provide that level of care if you don't know the work.

Software and hosting businesses have a number of characteristics that will affect how you carry out business. Never forget that you are actually running a business here. Regardless of how you structure your business to deliver your service, you are running a consulting, service, or hosting business (or some combination). That means you need to think carefully about marketing your business. You need to focus on developing systems for delivering your services. And you need to focus on developing systems for administering your business.

Like most consultancies and software development businesses, you need to have at least one customer to be a business. Never start a business until and unless you have your first customer ready, willing, and able to sign up with you. You need this income and the customer's active support in order to succeed.

Once you are up and running you are going to be faced with the labor wall. I'm talking about the fact that any labor based service -- and that's what we're talking about -- has distinct problems with scaling. You always purchase blocks of capability so there is a step-wise nature to your capability. As a result, you may find that you are unable to accept all the business that you can sell. To overcome this you need to always be thinking about how you can scale and reuse your services to expand your capabilities given your existing resources.

Up to this point most of the section reflects the fact that you will be running either a consultancy or a hosting business. However, blogging imposes several conditions of its own. The most important of these is the frequency of changes. Most blogging software providers release updates on an extremely frequent basis. This will impose strains on your business as you try to keep up with the effects of those changes. On the other hand, it also provides a number of opportunities. You need to be prepared for this constant and continual level of change.

Chapter 16:

Earning Around Blogging: Selling Products

What Is Earning Around Blogging by Selling Products

Of course, a service isn't the only thing about and around blogging that you can sell. There are a number of different products that can be sold. They form one of two different types of product.

The first type of product is a service that has been converted into a product in order to provide scalability. There are a number of different variations of this and most services can be converted. For example, an artist could create a number of blog designs and then sell the designs. Or a programmer could create a number of standardized blog packages and sell the package.

The second type of product is a direct result of the nature of blogging software. Most of this blogging software is designed to be easily modified. For example, most bloggers want a unique look and feel to their site. Typically, this is accomplished by a set of scripts called "themes". These themes control the color, font type, font size and placement of various elements within the blog. These customizations are packaged and can be sold either as a single design or as a modifiable set of functions.

In any case, selling these customization packages or products is basically the same as selling any other software. However, in this case, the blogging software project has a vested interest in ensuring that products are easily available. Therefore, they normally have some method of helping publishers connect with their customers.

What Can I Sell as Blogging Products

Selling blogging products is a very common way to monetize blogs and blogging. And the design of modern blogging tools allow you a number of possible ways to develop and sell products.

Most blogging software uses a theme to manage the look and feel. Many people are selling commercial versions of these themes. These are straight plug and play. Maybe you tweak it a little, change the graphics, or change the color scheme. But basically, it's plug and play.

And of course, people want their blogs to do things that aren't in the basic blogging software. So most of the software allows the installation of plug-ins. These are pieces of software that provide standardized customization. And of course, there are people who sell plug-ins to do just about anything that you need done.

Or you could sell an application. These are a predefined mix of theme and plug-ins designed to do specific tasks such as an e-commerce store or internet marketing or automobile advertising.

157

But it doesn't stop there. Someone has to create the theme, the plug-in and the application. And to do that, they need tools.   So you could always sell frameworks or development kits (aka SDKs) to create themes, plug-ins and applications.

Finally, you can let your customer off the hook for all of that by selling complete websites. Load and go. Some of these even have preselected keywords and domain names. The ultimate in "turnkey" or "done for you" solutions.

What Products Work Best as Blogging Products

Virtually anything associated with the blog can be packaged and sold as a product. Even content can be packaged as a product. This is what an article clearing house such as EzineArticles.com does.

However, generally speaking, the best products are those, which require specific skills such as programming. The reason being that those skills are not generally available. In order to get the desired functionality, people would have to pay a high price for custom work. By packaging the work as a product, you are able to sell the result for a lower price than any customized work could be provided.

How Much Can You Realistically Make with Blogging Products

The potential for income from products is extremely variable. The income pattern is precisely opposite to that of services. Because these products are sold for very small amounts, it is possible that your business will only earn the equivalent of advertising revenue. However, if you have a successful product, in theory the income could be enormous. Selling blogging products is a business. And like every business, it needs effort in marketing and in production. And it involves a certain level of risk and a large dose of uncertainty.

What Are the Advantages of Selling Blogging Products

Like any product sales, there are a number of different advantages to selling blogging products. I have already discussed many of these advantages. However, there are four big advantages that selling blogging products has.

Blogging products work extremely well when you are producing the products as part of a service or for your own use. This is because all of the costs are committed up front. Sales contribute only income. Once the initial commitment is paid for, the remaining income is profit. If you are able to recover the cost of development of the product from other sources, then most of your income will be profit.

The only exception to this is the cost of hosting and the cost of support. As the traffic increases, the blog supporting the products will need to be hosted on a series of increasingly expensive alternative hosting services. Similarly, the costs associated with providing support (answering questions, responding when problems occur etc.) also increase in a step-wise fashion.

This also means that blogging products are highly scalable. There are little or no production costs involved as the number of sales increases. Literally, the only increasing cost is the cost of hosting and support. Similarly, there is no limit to the number of copies you can supply. Or in the number of products, once your infrastructure has been established.

Making matters even better, is that there are a multitude of possibilities. Every user of the blogging software will have a variation on their requirements. Often you can use the same product with just minor variations to accomplish the job. Not only that, but there are several blogging software alternatives. All of this means that you can take one product and expand that to a suite of different products.

Finally, because much of the blogging software is developed through open source, the individual providers have encouraged community development. The providers can and will provide access for you to all customers who use their software. This greatly simplifies your need to market your products.

What Are the Disadvantages of Selling Blogging Products

Of course, selling blogging products is not a perfect business. There are a number of serious disadvantages. Not the least of which is, that this is a business not a get-rich-quick scheme. It will take you time, effort and money to build your sales to a viable level.

161

This market is very definitely based on the freemium model. You will need to produce free versions of your products and then find a way to build extra value to justify charging for the premium version.

Most of your competition will not have made the leap from freemium to premium. So your competition will be largely made up of individuals whose idea of income is a PayPal donate button. While they remain, they will disrupt your sales. Unfortunately, by the time they leave, someone else has joined to replace them.

Making matters worse, your clients will have learned to expect free product. So there will be a reluctance to pay money for your products. In most cases, this will be irrelevant. It merely removes those who are not potential paying clients from the mix. And the freemium model is based on providing sufficient value to push people to the premium product. However, sometimes this can result in a reduced price for the premium product. Your customers may feel that you should not be charging the price you have set. Sometimes, this is due to lack of value on the part of the premium service (compared to the free version). The problem comes in when it is the expectations of the customer that are out of synch with reality.

Finally, the biggest disadvantage is the frequency of change. WordPress for example, releases a major upgrade approximately once per year. However, it releases a number of interim upgrades (sometimes multiple times in one month). Even if your product is not affected, you will need to continually review and retest your product against these changes. At the least, you will then need to submit a new release showing the product as being compatible with the current release.

Hints, Tips and Gotchas of Selling Blogging Products

There are many rules if you are hoping to make selling blogging products a success.

First, and foremost is that you need to remember that this is a business. You are in the business of creating and selling products related to blogging. Your blog is only incidental to that business. And you need to run your business like a business. This includes identifying and utilizing multiple streams of supply and marketing. You can't just rely on the blogging software company to market your products. Like any business, marketing is a key element in your survival.

But this is a different type of business from most other product businesses. This is a business built on knowledge and skills. At the very minimum, you need to have knowledge of the platform you are building products for and knowledge of how products are built. If you don't have the knowledge, then you probably shouldn't be involved in this business.

Knowing what is involved is different from actually doing the work. There is no question that this business works best when you have both knowledge and skills. However, it is possible to hire the skills. It will however, be immensely more difficult to be successful if you do not have the skills necessary to do the work yourself. If you do not, then think very carefully before entering this business.

If you do decide to enter the business without the skills -- or if you just decide you don't want to do the work yourself -- it is possible to hire the skills. While you can hire the skills on a one-time basis, you will find that the maintenance load is such that extended partnerships are beneficial. After all, you don't want to turn a critical change over to someone you don't know.

While you have many options to locating those skills, there is one trick you need to take from the large players in outsourcing offshore. Large outsourcers always maintain two teams. The offshore team is given the responsibility to perform much of the development. The grunt work as it were. However, a local team is maintained to perform testing, and polishing. In this way, the end quality of the product is up to local standards and any communications issues can be overcome.

Finally, you need to be aware of and to be seeking alternate uses for your product. It is not always necessary to develop from scratch. Nor is it wise. Always be on the lookout for how you can tweak your products to be useful for other sets of customers. For example, if you are producing an application specific to lawyers, what do you have to do to turn it into an application for accountants? The answer may be as simple as new artwork and copy for a sales page.

Chapter 17:

Conclusion -- Bringing it all Together

Time to Make a Decision

Okay, so how do you actually choose one strategy over another? Or choose a number of strategies?

You can come into the process knowing what the decision is already.

Or you can use your purpose for the blog to determine the outcome.

Of course, your desires aren't the only reasons for making a decision. Sometimes your limits will restrict your choices, or direct the best choice.

For example, the amount of time available may mean that earning money from products or services isn't practical.

The amount of involvement you want to have may also direct your choices. For example, providing coaching or a service requires us to be heavily involved in providing that service. But you may not want to be heavily involved. So they may not be acceptable choices.

Of course, the amount of income you need the blog to produce may also affect the choice. I actually talked about that as I examined the alternatives and the hints.

Finally, the amount of traffic may affect your choices. Remember the cost equation? Unless you have the traffic to support it, the cost of providing services and product may be greater than the income you can derive.

Keep in mind that monetizing your blog is a matter of balancing diverse interests and developing a series of alternative income streams into the blog. The total money coming in needs to exceed the amount going out either in terms of time and energy or in terms of dollars.

Ultimately, that's the decision you are making.

Asking the Right Questions

There are no right and wrong ways to make your decisions. Nor is there a right or wrong answer. There is only your answer. And how you choose to reach a decision.

However, here is one way to decide by asking a series of five questions.

Do You Already Have a Business?

If the answer is no, then most likely, indirect blogging isn't for you. The only exception being if you are involved in Expert Marketing for yourself since you can use this to support seeking employment.

169

Do You Want to Run A Business?

If the answer is no, then most likely, earning indirectly and earning around blogging aren't for you. Again, the only exception being if you are involved in Expert Marketing for yourself since you can use this to support seeking employment. Additionally, earning directly by selling products or services is probably not suitable either. Most likely, the best strategies for you are selling advertising, commission sales, selling access, or a combination of those strategies.

Do You Know the Technology of Your Blogging Platform Well or Can You Learn It?

If the answer is no, then forget earning around blogging. The only possible exception is hosting blogs. With that service, the only knowledge you need is in how to use the blogging software and possibly what plug-ins to use.

Are You Prepared to Provide Premium Content Regularly (and Frequently)?

If the answer is no, then selling access to your content is probably not viable.

How Much Can You Realistically Make

Most of the "gurus" out there are selling you on how much money you can make. Most of the "gurus" just want to sell you on their next product. So they've got a reason for giving you unrealistic expectations. Most of us will never earn the types of bucks they are claiming. But ... you can earn a nice bit of extra income.

What could you do with an extra hundred dollars a month? That's one "Free" mortgage payment a year. Or it's half a car payment each month. It might even cover your electricity or heating bill.   The tax benefits alone might make it worthwhile.

Focus on making some money. Get started. Don't just dream about retiring to a beach. Or quitting your job. Get started even if there is only a few bucks a month coming in. It's going to take effort and time to build an income stream.

And hopefully it'll be fun along the way.

Here's the truth. No one can tell you how much you will make. It depends on too many factors. It depends on how tight your customer is. It depends on your pricing strategy. It depends on how much effort or money you put in. It depends on how successful you are in driving traffic. It depends on the products you have for sale. It depends on your business strategy.

Your income will vary. You can do two blogs exactly the same and have radically different results. There's a certain randomness to making money over the internet. So while I have tried to give you reasonable, relative amounts during this book, your own results will be all over the board. That includes income levels higher than my figures and income levels much less than my figures.

If I say a particular strategy is worth $100 month, you could easily find your results closer to $10. Or you could find your results somewhere in the $10,000 range. Not likely but it is possible. So the figures, I'm using are more to help you understand the relative values. And I'm basing them on what I feel is a reasonable number based on either reported averages or on my own experience. I'm also somewhat arbitrarily basing them on a thousand visitors per month. I hope that you'll do much better. But I won't be surprised if you don't.

On that same thread of thought, traffic is the key. If you are fortunate, lucky enough, or smart enough to pick the right micro-market you may find you have lots of traffic. If not, you're going to struggle. If you have enough traffic, then you'll make lots of money. If you don't you won't. That's why establishing and monitoring a set of metrics is so important. You need to know how responsive your micro-market is. And you need to test different techniques to get the greatest response.

That's also why building relationships with other bloggers and internet marketers is so important. They can be a major source of traffic for you.

That also leads to the next comment. There's no rule saying you're only allowed one blog. You can create as many of them as you wish. Each with a different strategy or business model or topic if you want. Or all with the same. You could create one blog to train people on how to be a contestant on Alec Trebeck's Jeopardy TV show and one on winning on "Let's Make a Deal". And another on building multi-stage rockets and satellites. (Yes, I'm being silly with my examples). Whatever you feel is appropriate. That's really what most of the "gurus" do. They have several sites each producing a few hundred

173

dollars or a few thousand dollars a month. They might have one that produces a hundred each month and another that produces a thousand. And so on. But at some point, they're raking in enough to make the job pay.

Let's say it takes you six hours a week to maintain one blog. I don't want to consider the time to create product so let's keep it simple. These will be pure content blogs with good free traffic. They will rely on other people's products and advertising to make money. That means you can maintain seven of those blogs in a normal workweek. If each of those blogs produced just $500 in advertising and commission revenue per month, you'd be earning $42,000 per year.

And that's very doable.

For more information on this topic visit our blog at http://www.howdoyoublog.biz

About the Author:

Glen Ford

Glen Ford is a co-founder and Chief Operating Officer with VProz Inc. He is a serial entrepreneur having set up the internet training company TrainingNOW and its subsidiaries as well as providing consulting services for startups in Debt Counseling, Software and Payment Processing. He has been principal of his own project management consultancy for over 11 years. During that time he has alternated his clients between government, the big banks and small to medium companies. Prior to that he spent 10 years working for the Canadian Standards Association and 10 years alternating between large distribution and manufacturing companies. Prior to that he worked for a very successful HVAC firm.

Glen is active in the business community as a member of The Project Management Institute (PMI) Lakeshore Chapter and a former training director for BNI Eagles Chapter of Business Network International (BNI). Glen is also an active supporter of charity including Scouts Canada (3rd Erin Mills Scouts). Glen holds a BSc from McMaster University in Hamilton, an

MCPM from York University (Schulich), and a PMP (Project Management Professional) designation.

Glen has been involved in the internet since 1995. He has been blogging since before content management systems such as WordPress existed.

TrainingNOW

TrainingNOW is a training and publishing company located in Mississauga *Training* NOW and Oakville, Ontario, Canada. It provides specialized web hosting services for companies seeking to deliver "how to" education over the web. It also publishes and sells "how to" books and training materials in digital, print and other media. Through its subsidiaries LearningCreators and ContentCreators it provides custom training material development. TrainingNOW maintains the following websites to provide specific training:

http://www.learningcreators.com provides training in learning content product creation (webinars, podcasts, books and eBooks).

http://www.howdoyoublog.biz
http://www.howtoblogmoney.com
and http://www.howtoblogcourse.com provide training on various aspects of writing and monetizing blogs.

Other Books By Glen Ford

How to Write Your Own How-To EBook in 24 Hours or Less: The Information Products Secret Revealed!
How to Document a Project Plan: What You Need To Know To Design A Project Management Plan Quickly and Easily

As Glen Douglas

How To Build A Raised Garden Bed

With Paul Benson

101 Limericks About Public Speaking

www.ingramcontent.com/pod-product-compliance
Lightning Source LLC
Chambersburg PA
CBHW061309220326
41599CB00026B/4797